P9-CMT-858

Special praise for *Dark Wine Waters*

"Fran Simone's finely drawn memoir offers testament that love is not enough against the disease of addiction. In sensuous detail, she traces the progression of her husband's alcoholism, the assault on a rich and loving marriage, and the ways they were twisted into strangers to one another and to themselves. This page-turner confirms that we are all more alike than different on the journey with an addicted loved one, and offers hope that the author's recovery can be our own."

Barbara Victoria, Author
It's Not About You, Except When It Is:
A Field Manual for Parents of Addicted Children

"Fran Simone has written a memoir that provides a powerful and insightful firsthand account of the disease of addiction. She chronicles the progression of not only the disease, but also the baffling progression of denial that engulfs the addicted person, leaving family members bewildered, angry, and hurt. I was inspired by her journey, her willingness to tell her story, and the miracle of hope that finds root in tragedy."

Ed Hughes, MPS, LICDC-CS, Author
Baffled by Addiction:
Successful Strategies to Help Your Addicted Loved One

AUG 0 1 2014

"You don't have to be an alcoholic to deal with alcoholism. This is a compelling account for anyone who has ever tried."

Charles Rubin, Author
Don't Let Your Kids Kill You: A Guide for Parents of Drug and Alcohol Addicted Children

---

"Simone vividly recounts her own compelling journey with the insidious disease of alcoholism and her sustaining spiritual awareness of recovery. *Dark Wine Waters: My Husband of a Thousand Joys and Sorrows* is both a tribute and an awakening to those who struggle with addiction and for those who love them."

Patrice M. Pooler, MA, ADC, Executive Director
Mid-Ohio Valley Fellowship Home, Inc.

DARK
WINE
WATERS

DARK WINE WATERS

MY HUSBAND OF A THOUSAND JOYS AND SORROWS

Fran Simone

CENTRAL RECOVERY PRESS

LAS VEGAS

Central Recovery Press (CRP) is committed to publishing exceptional materials addressing addiction treatment, recovery, and behavioral healthcare topics, including original and quality books, audio/visual communications, and web-based new media. Through a diverse selection of titles, we seek to contribute a broad range of unique resources for professionals, recovering individuals and their families, and the general public.

For more information, visit www.centralrecoverypress.com.

© 2014 by Frances Simone
All rights reserved. Published 2014. Printed in the United States of America.

No part of this publication may be reproduced, stored in a retrieval system, or transmitted in any form or by any means, electronic, mechanical, photocopying, recording, or otherwise, without the written permission of the publisher.

Publisher: Central Recovery Press
3321 N. Buffalo Drive
Las Vegas, NV 89129

19 18 17 16 15 14   1 2 3 4 5

ISBN: 978-1-937612-64-1 (paper)
          978-1-937612-65-8 (e-book)

Publisher's Note: Central Recovery Press offers a diverse selection of titles focused on addiction, recovery, and behavioral health. Our books represent the experiences and opinions of their authors only. Every effort has been made to ensure that events, institutions, and statistics presented in our books as facts are accurate and up-to-date.

This is a memoir, a work based on fact recorded to the best of the author's memory. To protect their privacy, the names of some of the people, places, and institutions in this book have been changed.

Dark Wine Waters is the story of a marriage affected by one partner's addiction to alcohol, and the text reflects both the subject's and the author's authentic experiences.

Cover and interior design and layout by Sara Streifel, Think Creative Design

To Terry D with love

Vitae Summa Brevis Spem Nos Vetat Incohare Longam

(The Shortness of Life Forbids Us Long Hopes)

They are not long, the weeping and the laughter,

Love and desire and hate:

I think they have no portion in us after

We pass the gate.

They are not long, the days of wine and roses:

Out of a misty dream

Our path emerges for a while, then closes

Within a dream.

Ernest Dowson

DARK WINE WATERS

Table of Contents

DARK WINE WATERS

Acknowledgments

Applause to Art Peterson, National Writing Project, for early encouragement, to Laurie Helgoe, my water muse, and the "Welty" writers, Cat Pleska and Barbara O'Bryne. To my many colleagues and students, especially the teachers and writers of the West Virginia Writing Project. Drum rolls for Rosanna Reaser, who provided valuable feedback and unstinting support during the manuscript's many incarnations. A standing ovation for Helen O'Reilly, CRP editor extraordinaire, whose comments and suggestions enriched my words. A chorus of gratitude to my twelve-step family and friends. Your experience, strength, and hope sustain me. Finally, to Simone E and Adam M, love always.

DARK WINE WATERS

Introduction

We know ourselves by the stories we tell. My story captures the progression of my husband's disease from the early, to middle, to late stages. I describe my husband's attempts to control his drinking and my attempts to control him. All of that was in vain, but we didn't know it at the time. Now I know better, and as I've learned in recovery, "if we knew better, we'd do better."

If writing is an act of discovery, then I came to know myself better as I wrote. Much of what I discovered about myself wasn't pretty. But as my story took shape, I found the courage to admit my faults, face my fears, and forgive my husband and myself. Though the hardships I endured seemed so personal, I now know that only the particulars are unique. This book is dedicated to all who know the joys and sorrows of loving an addict. My story is your story. My recovery can be yours as well.

PART I

Clear Water

THE ADDICT HAS A "WOW" EXPERIENCE AND

BEGINS TO FORM A RELATIONSHIP WITH THE DRUG.

FAMILY MEMBERS MAY OBSERVE SUBTLE CHANGES

IN PERSONALITY, AND A FORMIDABLE BARRIER TO

COMMUNICATION APPEARS: DENIAL.

DARK WINE WATERS

CHAPTER ONE

Setting Sail

I drank the water from your spring
and felt the current take me.

Rumi

I live in currents. I am often caught and carried to places other than where I thought I was headed.

That's how, at thirty-four years of age, I found myself waiting for my first date in eighteen years. A blind date, no less, because on impulse I'd called a stranger from Texas and invited him to my rented cottage in the woods, off a dirt road on a cold October evening in a town where I knew next-to-no-one. In retrospect, that wasn't wise. But I had misplaced my sense of propriety because I felt like a love-starved teenager who'd been dumped by her boyfriend.

I had recently moved to Charleston, West Virginia, with my five-year-old son, Matt, and a broken heart. My divorce loomed ahead. The push-pull of a breakup-and-makeup ten-year marriage had depleted much of my native goodwill and emotional energy.

One day my then husband announced "enough." He'd moved out of our home and in with his girlfriend, and purchased a Datsun 280 ZX. Armed with a new PhD, but toting a shattered ego, I couldn't decide whether to remain in Chapel Hill or look for a teaching position elsewhere. Back then, jobs in college English departments were in short supply. So I vacillated. My soon-to-be ex was a great dad who adored his young son. And I still loved him. But could I handle the humiliation of his shacking up with that other woman, a colleague from work? Chapel Hill is a small town and the university community even smaller. Stay, go. Go, stay. Then one day I decided to pop in on a friend to chew over the pros and cons of "the decision" once again. As I turned in to my friend's driveway, I spotted my husband's Datsun, alongside his girlfriend's red Volvo. *I bet they're splashing around in the backyard pool*, I thought. *Maybe hugging and kissing underwater like two lovesick teens, while I'm drowning in jealousy and fear.* My hands gripped the steering wheel. I shook and sobbed. I hit the gas and sped away.

The next day I began applying for jobs out of state. A current carried me to the heart of Appalachia, a place where I never would have imagined that I would wash ashore.

On a humid, late August morning, I slipped into a cool, dim auditorium for my first faculty orientation at a college in Stonehill, a coal mining town forty-five minutes from Charleston. As my eyes adjusted to the darkness, I spotted a striking-looking African-American woman near the back. She was dressed in black, with a kente cloth scarf draped around her neck. Her thin wrists were covered in silver bangles. *She looks interesting*, I thought, as I sank into a seat beside her. "You new, too?" I whispered. She smiled.

"Yes, my name's Marlene."

"Mine's Fran."

We turned toward the stage for the business at hand. Two hours later, Marlene and I plunged into the noon heat and fumbled for cigarettes and matches (Marlene was a light smoker, always on the verge of quitting; I consumed a pack of Salem Menthols a day).

"Did you understand even half of that stuff?" I wondered aloud. "Why do they have to go on and on about procedures and policies? Can't they just send us a memo?"

"Yeah, I'm still trying to figure out how I landed in Stonehill, West Virginia," Marlene said. "The place seems so backward and primitive."

Like starving animals, we gnawed at the college's deficiencies. Big city girls with attitudes—Marlene from Detroit, Michigan, and me from Queens, New York—we picked that campus apart over coffee and cigarettes in the faculty lounge during that first semester. Little escaped our scrutiny. Not the ancient campus buildings stacked like crates stuck onto the mountainside or the dank, musty offices in the administration building. Not the quirky faculty, like the humanities professor who kept a family of pet rabbits, all named Junior, in her cluttered office for many years. One cocky professor wore his Harley Davidson gear to class: black leather jacket complete with the logo, leather pants, boots, and long, stringy hair. It was rumored that this hell-raiser tried, with little success, to hit on eighteen-year-old coeds. And during lunch hour, a fraternity of staff members lumbered into the lounge, day after day, season after season, year after year, to play duplicate bridge.

Although the students from surrounding towns were earnest and friendly, many were unprepared, as evidenced by the abundance of remedial English and math courses offered each semester. I was assigned five sections of "Developmental English." Facing a class of twenty-plus students, many with brains but little preparation for college work, was a challenge, and I hardly knew where to begin. Not only did my students lack basic literacy skills, but many also lacked motivation, which was confirmed by their frequent absences and bogus excuses for missing class and turning in assignments late. During that first year of teaching, I treaded in rough pedagogical waters. But I learned more about teaching that year, from both my many failures and few successes, than during the subsequent thirty years (as I managed to stay afloat).

Both college and coal mines define Stonehill, sandwiched on a strip of bottom land between steep hills, adjacent to the Kanawha River. CSX trains carry coal along tracks that slice the town's midsection. Over the years, both the college and the mines had experienced a downturn.

During that first semester, Marlene and I figuratively picked over the male species like shoppers fingering fresh produce at a farmer's market. Each of us stood squarely at opposite ends of the love boat. Marlene was a blissful bride, and I, another casualty of divorce.

"What do you think my chances are of meeting a decent single male around here? Not that I'm quite ready yet."

"I hate to tell you, but things don't look too promising on this campus. Most of the male faculty are married. Then you have your total nerds and some weirdos. But there is a guy who works with my husband at Legal Aid. Just out of law school someplace in Texas. He's been here about a month. Came over to our apartment for a few beers after work last week. Kind of cute in a boyish way. Laughs a lot. Good sense of humor. And he doesn't have one of those funny accents."

A cute guy with a sense of humor? Okay . . . . But a Texan. Hhhmmm? I'd never set foot out West, with the exception of Los Angeles, which had overwhelmed me. My take on Texas was gleaned from grainy black-and-white cowboy movies that my father had watched on the old Philco TV back in our living room in Queens. Daddy sat wearing his clean white tee shirt, on the left side of our plastic-covered green couch, with a pack of Chesterfields on the coffee table, the hot ash of a half-smoked butt disintegrating in a lead-crystal ashtray. It seemed as if John Wayne starred in every Western. Those taciturn cowboys said, "Yup" and "Ma'am," wore ten-gallon hats, packed pistols, tied their horses to hitching posts, and fought in saloons. My dad loved to watch the good guys chase the bad guys. We cheered as the sheriff's posse sprang over chasms in a perfect arc from one mountain top to another in pursuit of the outlaws.

I tucked Marlene's Texan into the back of my mind as I raced to prepare my classes and settle Matt into kindergarten and our new mountain home. I lucked into a one-year lease on a furnished cottage while the owners, the Higginbottoms, spent a year teaching in Egypt. When I first came upon it, this shingled cottage glistened in the morning sun. Set deep in the woods, it reminded me of Snow White's house. Rather than the Seven Dwarfs, this abode was occupied by King, an elderly collie-shepherd mix. Soon King and Matt were inseparable, but I drew the line when Matt wanted to sleep with our rent-a-dog.

Matt and I spent a lot of time cooking, coloring, and reading books together in the kitchen with its long red Formica counter top and knotty pine cabinets. A baby grand piano dominated the small living room where a couch and a wing-backed chair, both covered in a yellow floral print, were arranged in front of a stone fireplace.

From the window above the kitchen sink, we watched sparrows, chickadees, finches, and cardinals land at the feeder in the yard. I kept a generous supply of suet and seed in the pantry. Matt was enthralled the day we spotted a family of white-tailed deer grazing in the front yard. During that year, I ran through three cords of firewood because cold air leaked through ancient casement windows. Later that year, we welcomed the warmth and colors of spring: trillium dotted the hillsides, forsythia twisted skyward, and jonquils graced meadows. There were also West

Virginia's ubiquitous, plastic Easter egg trees which delighted my son: "Oh, Mommy, can we get one of those trees for our yard?"

Although Matt missed his father, he adjusted quickly to his new school and surroundings. He adored his kindergarten teacher, Mr. Pauley, a gentle man who, with humor and love, tamed a rambunctious tribe of five-year-olds. Matt and his school buddies spent hours in the front yard climbing up, down, and around boulders that served as fortresses, jails, castles, and speedways, depending on the boys' fantasy of choice. They tussled with old King and raced their Hot Wheels up and down the gravel driveway.

I adjusted less well. I missed my friends, my comfortable contemporary home on its wooded lot on the outskirts of Chapel Hill, and the security of marriage, even one that had been unstable for several years. I still harbored faint hope that my husband and I might reconcile.

To help Matt during this difficult transition, I purchased a "special calendar" and marked each weekend that his dad would visit. Matt carefully placed a gold star on the date of each visit. Just after his bedtime story and before he went to sleep, he checked off each day, anticipating his dad's first trip in early October.

Matt's dad arrived on an unseasonably cold day, the kind with wood smoke in the air. As I opened the front door, Matt bolted toward his dad, who scooped him up, kissed his cheeks, and stroked his curly hair. After an awkward exchange with my soon-to-be-ex-husband, I handed Matt his Snoopy backpack, kissed him, and waved goodbye. Father and son departed in a rented car. I lingered in the front hall and faced my first weekend alone. More than forty-eight hours to fill. What to do? Best get busy.

I unpacked a few boxes, ran the vacuum, folded laundry, wiped down the kitchen cabinets, and walked King. Then I tackled student papers and littered the margins with "awk, frag," and question marks. I tried to untangle mangled English syntax. *What*

in the hell did these kids do during four years of high school English?
Around 5:00 p.m., I fixed a tuna sandwich and flipped through
the entertainment section of the newspaper. The Saturday
evening TV lineup wasn't promising; besides, reception on the
mountainside was no better than the grainy images on my dad's
old Philco. Normally a voracious reader, I couldn't concentrate
on what I judged to be the "fluff" in the Life and Style section of
the local newspaper about people and places I didn't even know
yet. I debated whether or not to phone my Chapel Hill friends
and dump more of my angst. Although I hadn't tired of venting,
surely they were tired of listening to me, swimming in circles over
my impending divorce.

An evening road trip, even to the local Mom-and-Pop
roadside store to pick up milk, wasn't feasible, as I feared driving
the winding roads that were covered in mud and littered with
ruts. What if my car careened into a ditch or a deer darted in
front of my headlights? Besides, I didn't need any milk.

Clearly my options were limited.

I didn't welcome the idea of another evening wrapped in a
bundle of regrets. So I smoked and paced, wishing I were anyone
but me, and anywhere but in this cottage on a dirt road five miles
from town and light years from Chapel Hill.

Then I recalled my conversation with Marlene about the
lawyer from Texas. In seconds, I shifted from idle into overdrive
and weighed the relative merits of contacting this total stranger.
*Would his phone number be listed? Could I call out of the blue? Was
that too pushy? Would I come across as needy?*

Then again, I *was* needy, and lonely too. But to admit it
was degrading.

Can I pull off "casual and confident"?

I reasoned that the Texan was new, maybe lonely too.

*Then again, he might have a girlfriend back home where the buffalo
roam, a former cheerleader or drum majorette. A beehived blonde with*

cowgirl boots and big boobs. But Marlene would have known if he was seeing someone. What's the worst that could happen? He might be a rube. Or some loudmouthed good ol' boy.

I'd heard that some of those Billy Bobs could be pretty insufferable about their allegiance to the Lone Star State. Maybe he went by initials only, like PC or JB, or worse yet, a nickname like Bubba. (When I first moved south, I'd met a Bubba Levy, so I knew it could be.) Then again, he might not be too keen on Yankees, let alone one with a New York accent. Could I—should I—dive in and phone this guy? So what if I'm blown off by the Texan? Could I handle another rejection? Rejection? I don't even know this guy! Enough, already. Either call the guy or forget about it.

And so I inched up to the phone, bit my finger, contacted the operator, gave her the Texan's full name, wrote down his number, took a breath, and dialed.

You will hang up after only five rings, I told myself.

He answered on the fourth.

"Um . . . hi . . . is this Terry? You don't know me but Marlene gave me your name and number. She said you were new here, too. I thought you might like to get together some time."

"Marlene? Oh, yeah, she's married to David from work. What was your name?" His voice was soft and smooth, without a trace of a Southern accent.

"Fran, my name is Fran. I'm teaching at Mountain Tech. That's where I met Marlene. We work together. I moved here from Chapel Hill last August with my son, Matt. He's spending the weekend with his father, so I was wondering if you might like to get together. It's the first cold night we've had and I'm planning to build a fire."

Am I crazy? Get together? Build a fire? What the hell is that supposed to mean?

"Well, I guess I could. I was supposed to meet some friends at a bar in town, but things got mixed up at the last minute.

Looks like I don't have anything else going, so I'm available. I live downtown. Where are you?"

Oh, God, here goes . . . don't let him be a serial killer . . .

"I'm renting a house up in the hills. On a dirt road, kind of out of the way. A few miles from town." *Great. If he is a serial killer, I'll make a terrific victim; the lonely college teacher, living up in the hills! Oh, Lord, what am I doing?*

But I pressed on.

"I'm not familiar with the roads around here. In fact, they scare me to death. And my sense of direction is pretty lousy. But I'll do my best with directions and hope you can find me."

"What time?"

"How about 8:00 or 8:30?"

"See you then."

Of course it was unwise, even dangerous, to have invited a complete stranger to my isolated home. But an impulsive current had overtaken me. I craved some male attention because, frankly, I no longer felt desirable. After all, my husband had flat-out rejected me. But as soon as I hung up the phone, I was tempted to call the stranger back and cancel. However, I was lonely, and didn't want to spend the evening alone, feeling sorry for myself. So emotions trumped reason, as they often did back then. Months later, Terry admitted, "You know after you called it crossed my mind that I might get lucky and score that night. Your invitation was mighty seductive." He grinned and patted my arm. I blushed.

I had two hours before his arrival. I ran water for a hot bath and soaked in bubbles. Then I powdered my skin, curled my hair, polished my nails, dressed and undressed. And re-dressed. Like a frazzled designer before a fashion show, I rifled through my meager wardrobe. Too baggy, wrong color, too formal, too flimsy, too hippie, too dowdy, too flashy. (Too tight wasn't a problem, as I was down to ninety pounds from my normal weight of 125, probably from the stress of the impending divorce.) I finally settled on a turquoise turtleneck, bell-bottomed jeans, plain gold hoop earrings, a gold bangle bracelet, beige socks, and tan sandals. After dressing, I pirouetted in front of a full-length mirror like a debutante. *Not bad*, I thought. The jeans fit snugly, but not too tight, and the nipples of my small breasts were visible beneath my shirt, but not brazenly. (This was during my—and seemingly the entire country's young, female population's—braless phase.) Understated, casual, "appropriate for the occasion," as my mother used to say.

As I carefully applied my powder, blush, a dab of mascara, and lip gloss, I felt like a fourteen-year-old on her first date. My *first date? Irish Teddy Riley.* We went to a movie in Flushing. *Exodus* with Sal Mineo? Or was it *Ben Hur* with Charlton Heston? Teddy from Brooklyn with his blond hair, blue eyes, and pug nose. After high school, he joined the army and was stationed at Fort Dix, New Jersey, for basic training. I started dating his best friend, Bobby. We wrote a few times, lost touch. Years later, my cousin Cosmo told me Teddy was a fireman, married, with a child. First date, first kiss, first love, you never forget them.

And now my first date in eighteen years.

Just before eight o'clock, I put a bottle of wine on to chill, built a fire, and fiddled with a stubborn curl as I checked and rechecked my image in a mirror.

8:30. The Texan didn't show.

9:00, 9:15, 9:30. Still no Texan.

I stared at the fire and cursed my impulsivity. I might have been dumped, but I'd never been stood up. Then again it might not be such a bad thing. After all, this guy could be a thug, a psycho, or a deranged vigilante like Travis Bickle in *Taxi Driver*. My embarrassment was tinged with relief. Maybe I'd been "asking for trouble," as my mother often warned me. These days, I'd kill one of my nieces for even contemplating such a move. But back then, I paced before the kitchen window, scanning the road for an approaching car. Seated briefly, I flipped through old magazines. Standing again, I poked resignedly at the dying fire . . . and then . . . .

A knock.

At 10:00 p.m. A smile. An apology.

"Hi. Sorry I'm so late. I really mean it. I got completely turned around in these hills and couldn't find my way back to the main road. Couldn't even find a house so that I could call you on the phone. No offense, but you live way out of nowhere. Look, I know it's late and I can leave right now. I'm really sorry about all of this."

"Well, I'd just about given up on you. Come on in, it's freezing out there."

Psychologists who study such things report that people feel positive or negative within seconds of a first encounter with a stranger. The reaction is visceral, immediate and, most times, permanent. My first impression was favorable: short guy, curly brown hair in need of a cut, kind amber eyes framed with wire-rimmed glasses, small hands, stubby fingers. He looked like a young Richard Dreyfuss without the nervous edge. Cuddly like a stuffed bear from my son Matt's animal kingdom. He wore faded blue jeans, scuffed white sneakers, a denim shirt, and a brown-and-beige checkered lumber jacket. His voice was gentle, without the trace of a Southern accent. A definite plus, for this Yankee. I detected a faint smell of Old Spice, which reminded me of my father. Another plus.

The Texan carried a six pack of Bud and a small paper bag.

We stood in the dim hallway and searched for words to wrap around those first awkward moments.

"Cold night."

"Yes, some frost. Didn't expect it so early."

"Nice place, but pretty far out."

"Yes, I got lost when I came to look at it to rent."

"You have a son? What's his name?"

"Matt. He's five, just started kindergarten. Great kid. I'll show you his picture."

He followed me to the kitchen and placed the beer and the bag on top of the worn Formica counter.

"Would you like a glass of wine or a beer?"

"Wine's fine, thanks."

As I poured two glasses from a half gallon of Gallo, he leaned against the counter and handed me the paper bag. "Here, this is for you."

"Oh, how nice. What a surprise," I bubbled. "I love surprises. Should I open it now?"

"Sure, go ahead."

Why did I ask him whether or not to open the bag? He must think I'm an idiot. Stop acting like a fourteen-year-old at a junior-high dance. What's in this bag anyway? Pot? I hope not!

I closed my eyes and warily slid my right hand into the bottom of the bag, cupped an object the size of a small stone, and fingered its smooth surface.

"I'm not sure. It feels small, and rounded, and kind of silky."

"Why don't you sneak a look?"

I opened the top of the bag, reached down, and grabbed a handful of . . . chestnuts.

"Thought you might like these. You said you were going to build a fire. You know 'chestnuts roasting on an open fire,' Nat King Cole?"

Curious gift, I thought. Not a bottle of wine, or a box of chocolates, or a pot of mums. *Chestnuts. This guy's thoughtful. And clever.*

He hooked me right in with those nuts.

For the next five hours, we sipped wine and outlined the surface of our lives, our conversation as seamless as the river that flowed through this mountain valley. We spoke of our childhoods, his in a suburb of Dallas, mine in a suburb of New York City. He spoke fondly of his undergraduate days at Austin College in Sherman, Texas.

"I graduated in 1971, in the middle of the war . . . "

"Oh. Vietnam . . ."

What was there to say about that terrible conflict?

"Um-hmm. I was about to be drafted. In fact, I was number five in the lottery."

I grimaced.

"You were in Vietnam?"

"No, no. Rather than go over there as cannon fodder, I went into a Presbyterian seminary in Louisville, Kentucky."

"You became a *minister* . . . ? I thought Marlene said you were a lawyer." I hoped I didn't look as confused as I felt. Terry smiled.

"No, preaching's not for me; I realized that after I spent some time working with some Catholic nuns in a poor section of town. But it was a stimulating experience. So I headed to Austin and law school at UT."

Then it was my turn. I told him about my extended Italian family, my Catholic education, and time at City College in New York. I rattled off the names of the grammar schools I'd attended, including the one called Fourteen Holy Martyrs.

"You're kidding, aren't you? That was the name of a school? What exactly did the fourteen of them do?"

"No, I'm not kidding. That was the name of the school. I have no idea what they did, probably burned themselves in oil or jumped from a mountaintop to avoid temptation of the flesh. The Catholics are big on temptation."

"So are the Southern Baptists. My mother used to send me to Sunday school at Walnut Hill Baptist Church."

"Sounds lovely."

"Well, it wasn't too lovely when they warned us that we'd surely land in hell if we drank and gambled. Guess it didn't take,

13

because I played a lot of poker when I was in college. Drank a whole lot, too."

We touched on geography.

"I grew up in Bayside, near Long Island. The ocean is in my blood. Someday I'm going to live by the sea."

"Then you'd better plan to head out of these mountains someday. You know, I didn't see the ocean until I was eleven. My mother and I drove from Dallas to visit relatives in Oregon. That was one of the few trips I took as a child."

"Not see the ocean until you were eleven? That's unbelievable. I'm a water baby. There's a picture of me at Coney Island when I was only eighteen months old. A pudgy little thing with a pot belly sticking out, carrying a pail and shovel. And my grandmother had a summer cottage on Long Island, so we went to the beach all the time. I took swimming lessons from the Red Cross when I was five. I still swim laps at the Y to keep in shape."

"Must work. You look pretty good to me."

A surge of delight washed over me like a gentle wave, even though I had pretty much invited that compliment. But he hadn't disappointed.

Terry mentioned the "big sky" out West. "I sure miss that."

"All I know about the West is from the Westerns I watched with my dad when I was a kid. I've never been out there."

Suddenly, Terry was gone, replaced by a pretty good John Wayne impersonator. "Now, missy, let's get this straight," he drawled, exactly like the Duke, even pushing an imaginary cowboy hat further back on his head, and hooking a thumb into his belt. "I'm partial to those movies too. After all, I'm a Texan, and damn proud of it." (Like every Texan I've ever met, he felt entitled to bragging rights.)

This charming stranger could certainly make me smile.

And when Terry "returned," we talked about our recent moves to West Virginia and speculated about how long we might stay.

I rambled on too long about my impending divorce. He didn't interrupt me. "Mind if I get another beer?" he asked.

I learned that he was a movie buff who favored classics like *The Wizard of Oz, It's a Wonderful Life, Citizen Kane,* and *The Maltese Falcon.* It seemed that movie stars like Tracy, Bogart, Gable, Jimmy Stewart, and Cary Grant were as real to him as the trees that rustled outside the living room window.

"I actually wanted to go to UCLA to study film, but that seemed unrealistic for a poor kid like me. Also too risky. Not enough security."

"You're still young. Maybe you'll change careers and go. I read somewhere that people might change careers three times in a lifetime. Are you sorry you became a lawyer?"

"Well, I'm no Perry Mason. But I'm not too shoddy either. I don't make piles of money at Legal Aid, but I feel good about what I do. Poor people deserve to be represented. Besides, my office is clean and well lit." He winked.

I later discovered that this sensitive child of an alcoholic had mastered the subtleties of nonverbal body language. This served him well in court and at poker games with his cronies. I soon learned that everyone who met Terry was warmed by that self-deprecating humor and calm, courteous manner that was charming me so on that first night. "Yes, sir" and "no, ma'am," were part of his appeal.

Bathed in firelight, we lay on pillows in front of the fireplace and gorged on crackers, cheese, and conversation. When the fire faded, Terry hauled logs from the woodpile beside the kitchen door and carefully arranged them on top of the embers. Our eyes danced in the shadows of flickering flames. He sprinkled a fistful of chestnuts in a metal pie plate to roast in the fire. Once they had roasted and cooled, he peeled one and placed it carefully in my mouth. As I tasted the warm, grainy inside of the nut, Terry's fingers brushed against my cheek. Then he circled the outline of my lips with his index finger and stroked my chin. He leaned forward to kiss me. Sweet, gentle, innocent.

Slightly embarrassed, we chuckled like kids caught in their own delight. Not sure of what to do next, I headed to the kitchen to replenish cheese and crackers. Terry followed and gathered more logs. We repositioned ourselves in front of the fire. Surely soft music played in the background, but I can't recall a song or melody. Perhaps Johnny Mathis or Nat King Cole.

"Oh, my God. It's so late; it's almost 4:00 a.m.," I said.

"Guess it's time for me to be leaving. You won't mind if I take this last beer with me? One for the road."

As we stood face-to-face in the dim light of the entry hall, he whispered, "Can I kiss you again?" He lifted my chin, leaned down and kissed my lips. Again, sweet and tender. Then he grabbed his lumber jacket and opened the front door. As he turned to leave, he saluted me like Bogart.

"Here's to you, kid." He cocked his head and grinned. "Let's do this again, sweetheart."

I lingered in the hall, watching as he walked up the front path toward the road. Then he climbed into his ancient Plymouth Fury and revved the engine. Gravel rattled. My heart raced.

I tossed the empty beer cans into the garbage and thought, boy, that guy drinks a lot of beer. Then I glanced at Matt's calendar. October 3—a gold-star day.

CHAPTER TWO

Sea of Desire

It is difficult to know at what moment love begins;
It is less difficult to know that it has begun.

Henry Wadsworth Longfellow

A month later on a brisk, cloud-free day, Terry and I walked hand-in-hand through downtown Charleston, heading for his apartment. Our conversation turned to his junior year abroad in Copenhagen in 1970.

"I loved it," he said. "My first time away from Texas, except for that trip to Oregon with my mother I told you about. I explored the breweries and drank huge amounts of free beer. My research project, so to speak. I chased after young women, without much success. Austin College had some connection with an international school there. Mainly we'd sit around and shoot the breeze in so-called seminars. We had plenty of time to travel. I bought a scooter and ran around with a classmate. Guy named Aubrey. We went to France, Italy, Sweden. Stayed in youth hostels and cheap hotels. I had very little money."

"Wow! Europe. I've never been," I pushed a strand of hair behind my ear. "One of my college friends was born in Italy. She used to visit relatives. My grandparents emigrated from Sicily." The words were pouring out of me, from nervousness, or embarrassment, or some combination of both. "Don't think anyone from the family still lives there. I'd love to go to Italy. Heck, I'd like to go almost anywhere, but especially Europe." If my nervous rush of talk bothered him, he didn't show it.

"I didn't get to stay in Denmark for a full year like I planned," he went on. "Everything ended when my scooter crashed. I broke my left leg."

"Oh, how awful!"

He grimaced ruefully.

"When I tell you how, you have to promise you won't laugh."

"Why would I laugh?"

"'Cause I was hit by a sausage truck."

I cackled. He smiled and gently punched my shoulder.

"I asked you not to laugh." But he was smiling. "Anyway, the doctor didn't set my leg right. I stayed in Dallas for a while and then I hobbled around campus in a weird metal contraption."

During the year that Terry had been scooting around Europe, I'd been immersed in motherhood: breastfeeding Matt at 2:00 a.m., changing diapers, and delighting in my baby boy's milestones, his first smile, coo, babble, word, and step.

But Europe! Images danced through my mind. Elsa and Rick riding in a convertible through the French countryside in *Casablanca*. Princess Grace in her Monaco palace. Scott and Zelda cavorting with wealthy expatriates and artists on the Riviera. Audrey Hepburn and Albert Finney hitching rides in *Two for the Road*.

Me? Hitching rides? Out of the question.

"Here I am thirty-four-years-old and I've never been to Europe."

"Oh, you'll get there someday."

Terry told me that a friend from college, Diane, had spent a year in France, where she met her future husband, Jacques, while hitchhiking. After graduation she moved to Paris to marry. Back then most of us married right after graduation.

Instead of hitching rides through Europe, I'd married my high school sweetheart, Anthony, in 1964. High Mass at my parish church, St. Kevin's, and a lavish reception at Leonard's of Great Neck. We'd headed south to Gainesville, Florida, where he worked on a PhD in sociology and I returned to school for a master's degree. Our son, Matt was born in 1970.

"So was Paris as romantic as in the movies?"

"Yeah, like *An American in Paris*. You remember that one?"

"Gene Kelly, dancing with Leslie Caron . . . in the fountain spray, from the *Place de la Concorde* . . . how could I forget?" Terry grinned at my enthusiasm, whether for Paris or for the film, I'll never know. Encouraged, I went on, now in full spate.

"I've got an idea. Maybe we could go to Paris this summer and stay with your friends. It wouldn't cost that much if they'd put us up. Anthony has Matt for six weeks this summer. And I'm teaching only one class the first semester. So I'm free for a whole month." Terry's brow furrowed comically, but I was barely getting started, and my ideas were flowing out in a torrent.

Back then, I free-floated in a mist of mania, a "go-for-it" mindset of magnificent possibilities—including a trip to Europe with my friend and lover. My wanderlust wasn't new, but I hadn't previously had the courage or opportunity to act on it. When I was seventeen, I'd begged my parents to send me away to college, but they wouldn't hear of it. "Frances, where do you get these ideas?" they asked, genuinely puzzled by my desire to leave home. Back then young women in traditional Italian families didn't leave home until they married. Period. No exceptions. So I lived at home and matriculated at City College. My father placated me by offering to pay half the cost of a car if I earned the other half. I worked part time at Lord & Taylor's department store and saved my money. During my sophomore year, I saved enough to purchase half of a shiny, new, bright blue Mercury Comet. Not long after graduation, I married and headed south, eventually landing in Chapel Hill, a pleasant enough town. It had been nice. But it hadn't been Paris.

"What do you think of going to Europe? Is the idea too outrageous?" I asked.

Terry smiled but let go of my hand. He bit his upper lip.

"No offense, Frannie, but how do you know that we'll even be dating next summer? It's pretty far away. Besides, I probably can't afford it. And I might not be able to get away from work."

Undaunted, I plunged right off the high-dive. As if I were the trained lawyer, I laid out a reasoned argument. One, plane tickets were cheap; two, food was inexpensive (a loaf of bread, a jug of wine, and thou); three, Terry's friends in Paris would probably put us up, and if not, we could stay in hostels and *pensiones*. (Although this was the era of "Europe on Ten Dollars a Day," the idea of backpacking, though it would have been even cheaper, wasn't an option for me.)

"Frannie, I can't imagine you staying in a hostel. Your idea of camping out is a room at the Holiday Inn."

I pushed ahead.

"Well, at least think about it. If, for some reason—and I can't imagine what that would be—we break up, or something comes up, then we cancel. People cancel all the time."

Since I knew Terry loved to gamble, I pulled out the ace of spades.

"You know, after Paris we could drive south to Monte Carlo. Visit the palace. You could gamble at the casino. Try your hand at blackjack or roulette."

He changed the subject.

"You thirsty? Want something to drink?"

Once at his apartment he drank beer, I drank Coke, and we made love for the rest of the afternoon.

Years later when we dug out photos from the trip, Terry said: "Remember that day we first talked about going to France? You came on pretty strong. Pushy New YAWK-er. And guess what? Turns out you are." He grinned, raised a Bud, and saluted me. "You know I'm only kidding."

"You'd better be."

On July 20 of the year following our first meeting, Marlene and David were waving good-bye to Terry and me at the Kanawha County Airport. Terry and I were boarding a puddle jumper to Pittsburgh for a connecting flight on Icelandic Airlines. In Reykjavík my feet hit foreign soil for the first time. In terms of our relationship, however, it was as if we had crossed the Atlantic Ocean only to land on the shore of another sea; the Sea of Desire.

But as that day began, Terry and I trudged behind other weary passengers to the duty-free shop. I sifted through bins of hand-knitted sweaters, scarves, and gloves and purchased purple mittens for Matt and two cartons of Salem Menthols for myself, and Terry carried two bottles of Johnnie Walker Black Label and Cuban cigars back to the plane.

Hours later, we arrived at the tiny airport in Luxembourg. Anticipating jet lag, I had booked us into what was, for us, an expensive downtown hotel. After surrendering our passports at the front desk, we followed a porter to an elegant room—high ceilings, enormous bed, ornate headboard, plush duvet, and heavy drapes in rich mauve. A chandelier glistened overhead. His-and-her bathrobes hung in the closet. This was no hostel. I untied the heavy drapes, pushed open the shutters and gaped at the pedestrians strolling in the park below. Terry ordered ice and poured himself a tall glass of whiskey.

"Terry, come look. It's . . . charming, like I imagined."

He reached around my waist with one arm, while with the other he raised his glass.

"Here's to you, kid."

We held hands and lingered at the window. I ran a bath, and, like every American encountering one for the first time, felt compelled to make a comment on the bidet.

Steam soaked the mirrors and the black-and-white tiles as we sank into a claw foot tub. Like children, we splashed, played footsie, and soaped each other's backs.

"I can't believe I'm here. I feel as if I'm in a movie," I said.

"Not too shoddy," he said as he raised another glass of Johnnie Walker. Wrapped in thick terrycloth robes, we tumbled onto the king-size bed and nestled beneath the thick duvet. We quickly shed our robes, and some time later, as I basked in the afterglow of lovemaking, Terry fixed another drink.

"You want one?"

"No, I'm fine. But I'd like some water. Do you think it's okay to drink from the tap?"

The next morning, we slept late, skipped breakfast, and fondled one another in the shower.

"How about it?" Terry asked. As he pressed himself against me, it was apparent that he was definitely ready. But I demurred.

"Not if we want to check out on time." I ventured coyly. Who was I kidding? I was as ready as he was.

So it was some time after checkout that we loaded our suitcases into a tiny aquamarine Renault and headed toward Paris.

"You drive," I offered. "I'll navigate." I unfolded a map and Diane's letter with directions to her apartment, located in the 20th Arrondissement on the eastern edge of the City of Light.

We drove in what we hoped was the right direction, but encountered road and street signs we couldn't decipher. The feeling of disconnect due to the language barrier was something

I hadn't anticipated. Terry clutched the steering wheel and maneuvered the Renault through heavy traffic. Other tiny cars were parked bumper-to-bumper; many straddled the space between the curb and sidewalk, if there was a curb at all.

"You know, this is like driving in Manhattan during rush hour. Only the cars are smaller. And if New York drivers parked their cars on the sidewalk, the cops would tow them in a heartbeat," I said.

I was fumbling with the map as we entered the city limits. Utterly lost and confused, I yelled,

"Lions at a gate! Diane wrote something about statues of lions at a gate as we enter the city."

Terry hunched forward frantically and gripped the wheel.

"Frannie, this isn't a safari."

But somehow, there they were, lions! After many wrong turns, somehow we'd stumbled upon the right apartment building. We parked the car as Jacques, Diane's husband, held open the wrought-iron gate. He was a gregarious giant with jet-black hair, friendly eyes, and the prominent nose of a de Gaulle or a Sarkozy.

"Ter-ree. Bienvenue, bienvenue. Come, come." He helped carry our heavy luggage through a sunless courtyard and up three steep flights of stairs.

Diane opened the door to their tiny apartment and greeted us in her husky voice, "Come, come, so good to see you. Did you have any trouble finding us?" She and Terry hugged. A tall, bone-thin blonde with blue-green eyes and pale skin. Next to willowy Diane, I felt like a frump. As we crossed the threshold, I spied a bare mattress that covered the entire living room floor. Terry and I would sleep there, while Jacques and Diane squeezed into a daybed tucked into an alcove. This lack of privacy did not inhibit our lovemaking. When Jacques and Diane headed for work, Terry and I headed for the mattress. Some days, we spent as much time exploring one another as we did touring that magnificent city.

During our five-day stay, we lingered for hours at the small table set beside a window facing a courtyard, and drank wine that had been made by Jacques's father, who lived in Sorède, a tiny village in the Pyrénées. Diane and Terry reminisced about college: oddball professors, old friends, silly pranks, bull sessions, and times when the beer flowed and pot perfumed the air with its sweet smoke. Jacques cooked extravagant omelets and served generous portions of crusty bread, croissants, pâté, cheese, and pastries. (He taught me to make authentic French dressing and mayonnaise.) I switched from Salems to Gauloises. Terry developed a taste for Courvoisier, and he and Jacques sampled the Cuban cigars Terry had purchased in Reykjavík.

Jacques spoke little English and my high school French was abysmal. I had mastered a few phrases like, *"Ou puis-je charger des chèques de voyage?* Terry memorized, *"Avez-vous une bouteille de whisky?"* He complained about warm beer and the lack of ice cubes in drinks. At a local café, Jacques roared when I wanted a Coke but ordered *un coq* (rooster). Diane toggled between French and English, speaking each with a faint Texas drawl.

The four of us squeezed into the Renault, and Jacques whisked through Paris traffic with the skill only a native can possess. We visited famous landmarks: Notre Dame, the Eiffel Tower, the Louvre, and newly opened Pompidou Center built on the site of the Old Paris marketplace, Les Halles.

"It looks like a giant erector set," Diane commented. "I hate it and so do most Parisians."

Like countless lovers before us, Terry and I held hands as we strolled along the Seine.

"Not like the Kanawha back home," I mused. "Much more romantic." He purchased a pen-and-ink drawing of Notre Dame, which now hangs in the front hallway of my home. We purchased souvenirs for Matt, a six-inch replica of the Eiffel Tower, a tiny French flag, and a snow globe of Notre Dame. At Versailles, I snapped a picture of Terry standing in front of a palace window in soft light, looking down at a tourist guide. It's one of my favorites. At the Sunday flea market, Jacques bargained with an African vendor for a cloisonné bracelet. I wear it still.

When Jacques wasn't cooking, he'd whisk us to his favorite restaurants.

"Tonight, you are in for a treat. We made a reservation at Androuet's, which specializes in cheese."

Maneuvering around tables jammed together, busy waiters hoisted huge trays of cheese: mild, sharp, pungent, spicy, moldy, and creamy. Cheeses sculpted into cones, spheres, triangles, and pyramids. Jacques painstakingly selected an assortment and ordered a bottle of wine. At one point, Terry quipped, "*Est-ce que la Velveeta?*" Hours later, we emerged, bellies full, arteries clogged, and heads spinning from too many bottles of red wine.

The night before our departure, Jacques and Diane helped us plot our course through the Loire Valley toward the Mediterranean. Then we lifted the mattress from the floor and propped it against the wall. Jacques placed a recording of Georges Brassens on the turntable and we danced late into the night in that miniscule space.

Early the next morning, we lugged suitcases, bread, cheese, and homemade wine downstairs and packed everything into the Renault. Just before we left, I snapped a picture of Terry and Jacques standing arm-in-arm, sporting black berets in front of an iron gate. That black-and-white photo sits on the windowsill in my study today. Jacques and Diane waved goodbye.

"*Bonne chance. Au revoir.*"

Coming down from the exultant high of Paris, I sank into the passenger seat and closed my eyes. Terry leaned over and said, "Well, kid, now we can say that we'll always have Paris."

Yes. Just like Elsa and Rick (but without their troubles), Terry and I fell in love in Paris. Our romantic scenes could have been scripted for a French film. Many of them seemed lifted straight from the movies. Terry and I strolling along the Seine, holding hands, stopping to hug and kiss; sipping wine at an outdoor café in sun-sparkled light; snapping photos of one another in the gardens of Versailles; purchasing souvenirs at the flea market. Yes, indeed, whatever misfortunes occurred in the future (and who could imagine any misfortune occurring to such a couple as ourselves), we would always have Paris. Who wouldn't be grateful for such memories?

As we made our way through the Loire Valley, I noted famous cathedrals and opulent *châteaux*, including Chartre, Chenonceau, and Chambord in my journal.

After several days of such ornate lavishness, Terry gave out.

"No offense, Frannie, but this Texas boy is about *châteaued* out." The fact is that we were more interested in savoring the sensual delights of one another than in learning which Medici, Duke, Baron, or Pope had resided in which castle, château, or cathedral during which period of the early, middle, or late Renaissance. "What do you say we head back to the hotel and fool around?"

"I say that's a terrific idea."

At Néris-les-Bains we joined elegant elders, fresh from the mineral baths, as they promenaded in a central square. "Terry, look at that couple. So fragile. Like fine porcelain. Do you think that years from now we'll stroll arm-in-arm like that?"

"At their age we'd be lucky to hobble on this terra firma."

"Together?"

"Maybe so, Frannie, maybe so."

Outside Aubenas, we picnicked on wine and cheese at a cemetery.

"Soulful spot; no pun intended," Terry said.

We wandered among tombstones, trying to decipher names and dates that had been eroded by time.

"So how do you plan to dispose of your remains when, God forbid, the time comes?" I asked.

"Well, I know one thing; I don't plan to become fodder for the worms. I want to be cremated. My Southern Baptist mom won't cozy to the idea. Hopefully, she'll never know. No matter. When you're dead, you're dead."

"So what are your thoughts on an afterlife? Heaven? Purgatory? Karma? Sister Margaret Mary used to scare me to death about purgatory. And limbo. I could never understand that one."

"Eternal life. That's one of those many metaphysical mysteries. Like when the Dallas Cowboys have a lousy season."

"Do you believe in soul mates?"

His amber eyes told me the answer as he brushed his hand against my check. A rush of pure pleasure shot through my body.

"What do you think?" he answered.

We arrived at Aix-en-Provence at lunchtime. "Golden," I wrote in my journal. Light filtered through tree branches that lined Cours Mirabeau, reputed to be the most striking boulevard in Europe. At a crowded outdoor café, we savored omelets and crusty bread. Terry ordered a bottle of white wine. Between courses we held hands across the table.

When the waiter started to pour, I cupped my hand over the glass.

"*Non?*"

"Thanks. It's too early in the day for me," I said too loudly, as if by shouting I could make the waiter understand English.

"Terry, this place is beautiful. It's my favorite so far."

"Frannie, you've said that in about every town we've visited. I hear tell that those towns along the Med—eye—terrean aren't too shoddy. Yachts, villas, the rich and famous; your cup of tea."

When the waiter placed the bill on the table, Terry fumbled with a wad of francs and tipped over the wine bottle. I was momentarily startled, but I needn't have been. It was empty.

I remember thinking, *That's a great deal of wine to drink in such a short time.*

The Riviera. This hedonist's heaven pulsed with tourists and traffic. Villas spilled down sloping hillsides toward the sea, where yachts bobbed in the harbor. Clinging crimson bougainvillea draped itself around stone walls, and a parade of palm trees nodded gracefully under an azure sky. All of this was bathed in brilliant light. But the brightest light casts the deepest shadows, and that's where I fancied Scott and Zelda lingered.

When I was fifteen, I'd discovered F. Scott Fitzgerald while browsing in the Queens County Public Library, Bayside Branch. Why I happened to grab a copy of *Tender Is the Night* is still a mystery. I'm certain the nuns at Bishop McDonald High School didn't assign any of Fitzgerald's novels, not even his classic, *The Great Gatsby*, which I read in college. I fell hard for Scott and Zelda and their friends, Gerald and Sara Murphy. I pictured them cavorting with the artistic crowd at the Villa America near Cannes. I cheered their extravagant life style and suffered their pain and heartbreak. Such sophistication, such drama, such tragedy. *Nothing like that ever happened in Queens.*

Terry and I settled in at the Hotel des Fleurs in Menton. "Terry, come look, what a view. I've changed my mind about my favorite place. This is it. Definitely. *La mer, la mer*, the sea, the sea." *And there we were, swimming in our own sea of desire for one another.*

"Maybe you should wait for Italy before you decide. After all, it's the motherland of your ancestors. You should feel right at home. Better yet, why not make it easy and pick your top ten. How about a drink?"

"No thanks. I'll stick with mineral water. You know, with gas."

Once again, we lingered in a steamy bath. Once again, he downed several tumblers of scotch. Once again, we made love. One evening, we strolled into the courtyard of an ancient church and held hands as the melody of one of the Brandenburg Concertos soared over the sea toward the stars. As we turned to leave, he offered his arm in a courtly gesture.

"Well Frannie, I do believe that living well *is* the best revenge."

"It sure as hell is," I replied.

The next morning, while visiting the Jean Cocteau wedding chapel in the Town Hall, Terry was silent. *Was it fatigue? Was it too early in the morning? Did I say something wrong? Did the proximity to the nuptial chapel unnerve him?* At the time, I didn't recognize that he was hung over. And even if I had, I would have dismissed it.

So what if he drank too much last night? Everyone indulges on vacation. And in Europe, wine is water.

So began my denial and rationalizing, in hope and innocence.

Terry perked up as we ambled toward a crowded outdoor market loaded with fresh fish, cheese, meats, veggies, herbs, and flowers.

"Oh, my God. All of this fresh food. And the variety. It's nothing like Kroger back home."

"Frannie, I have to make a pit stop. You go ahead and I'll meet you at that café across the street."

Minutes later he reappeared with an enormous bouquet of fresh-cut flowers.

"*Pour vous, mademoiselle.*"

"*Merci, mon amour.*"

In subsequent years, Terry often brought me small gifts, especially after he drank too much. A big bar of Toblerone, a bottle of Chanel cologne, or a dozen yellow roses. One time, after days of stone silence, he outfoxed me with a bag of chestnuts.

But all of that was in the far future. I didn't know then that this was a preemptive peace offering, prompted by his alcoholic's sense of guilt. No, on that sun-filled day in an outdoor café in the south of France, I simply accepted it as a token of new love, and Terry and I glowed with desire like the snapdragons in my innocent bouquet.

I scrutinized the menu. "Ah, *bouillabaisse*. Fish stew. Let's try it."

When a waiter set a pot of broth and gigantic platter of fish before us, Terry gasped.

"No offense, but I can't eat anything with dead eyes staring at me. This is definitely not my kettle of fish. No pun intended. Give me chicken-fried steak any day. You want another beer?"

That afternoon, he nursed several scotches as we rested before our planned adventure at the casino. He wobbled as he headed for the shower. However, it wasn't long before, smelling of scented soap, he emerged refreshed, and dressed carefully in the new sports coat and red silk tie that I'd purchased before we left home. I sparkled in a black sheath covered with sequins.

"Smashing. Don't you think? We look absolutely smashing," he said. He bowed slightly and held out his arm. We glided out the hotel door like Fred Astaire and Ginger Rogers stepping onto the dance floor.

The casino was Old-World elegant: stately women with smooth, tanned skin wrapped in satin and chiffon, their diamond (or maybe they were rhinestone) necklaces shimmering, and their lacquered hair fashioned into elaborate twists or chignons. They were flanked by men in well-cut suits and tuxedos. I wouldn't have been surprised to discover James Bond sipping a dry martini at the bar. The ornate salons glimmered under massive chandeliers. Although suitably dressed, I felt out of place. At the craps table I edged between gamblers who tossed fistfuls of multi-colored chips onto the, green felt. When we managed to secure a spot at the table, Terry tried to explain the combinations, the "Pass," "Don't Pass," "Hardways," "One Roll bets," and the like, but the game was too fast for me. So I joined a pack of gamblers at the slot machines. Within minutes the machines had swallowed my meager stack of coins. Meanwhile, Terry checked out the private gaming room reserved for the rich and reckless.

Saving for months before the trip, Terry had squirreled away several hundred dollars, a minimal stake intended to allow him to cavort with the high rollers in the *salons privés*. He went off to try his luck at Twenty-One and tapped out in less than an hour.

"You lost it all? I'm sorry. I know how much you were looking forward to this."

"No big deal. Never wager more than you can afford to lose, Frannie. That's my motto. Besides I have a few *francs* left. Let's find a bar and get a few drinks."

If only his drinking had been conducted like his gambling. He knew when to stop gambling, and he did. If he budgeted five hundred dollars for one evening, he quit when he lost his stake. Most times he won or broke even, especially when he played poker.

"It's not solely about the money," he insisted. "I like to be ahead because I can stretch it out. It's more about having fun and trying to beat the odds."

"Fat chance of that," I replied.

———

Several weeks after we returned to Charleston, I received a postcard in a familiar handwriting—Terry's—from Bellagio, Italy. The inscription read: "This is paradise. Aren't we having a good time? Love, T."

We almost hadn't ended up at Bellagio. From Menton we'd driven along the coast to San Remo where terraced fields of roses, carnations, and camellias filled the hillsides. Our bliss, however, was temporarily punctured in Genoa. I don't recall exactly what happened. Perhaps I made some remark about his drinking, but

I do remember how we sat at opposite ends of an empty city tour bus, pouting like three-year-olds.

Later that day, we declared a truce as we packed the Renault and headed toward Lake Como.

"Frannie, it's been a long day. I'm tired. Why don't we stop in Como and spend the night?"

"I want to get to Bellagio today. I read a description in the AAA guide. It's the town on the peninsula that divides the two sides of Lake Como. Outstanding hotels and restaurants. Plenty to see. So what do you think?"

"I think you already made up your mind. How long will it take to get there?"

"The guidebook says about twenty-seven kilometers. What's that in miles? I always get confused."

"It's about fifteen. But no telling how long it'll take on these roads. They're like back home. And you aren't a very good navigator."

"I'll do the best I can. It'll be worth it. You'll see." I hoped that my enthusiasm for the town would rub off on Terry, and that the AAA guide wasn't exaggerating.

As the Renault chugged up a narrow, winding road with hazardous switchbacks, Terry looked straight ahead and gripped the steering wheel. We almost wrecked when an Italian driver in a red sports car blew his horn to signal a blind curve a second before the car shot through a hairpin turn.

"*Basta.* Italian drivers. Goddamn. Unbelievable."

Later that afternoon, our driving nerves were soothed, as we settled into an elegant room at the Hotel Florence where we were mesmerized by our view of the lakefront. All reluctance and annoyance forgotten and swallowed up in the view from our windows.

Our guidebook recommended visits to the Basilica of San Giacomo, the gardens of the Serbelloni Villa, the chapel at

Villa Melzi, and other "must see" sites. We wound up and down steep stone steps past iron balconies festooned with clay pots of red geraniums or laundry drying under the hot sun. At the many shops tucked below apartments, we admired fine silks and Venetian glass jewelry. I purchased a tee shirt for Matt and silk scarves for Terry's mother and aunt.

We drank wine at a café on the lake and sampled food cooked in heaven: lake trout, perch, fluffy risotto, and ripe white peaches. Our lovemaking became another delicious taste to savor, and savor it, we did.

Like the excursion boats slowly crisscrossing the surface of the lake, we floated in a perfect dream. In my journal I wrote: "I'm totally happy."

So was the composer Franz Liszt. In 1837, while cavorting with the Countess d'Agoult, he wrote, "When you write the story of two happy lovers, set them on the shores of Lake Como. I know of no other spot more obviously blessed by heaven."

Bellagio soared to the top of my "most favorite" list. *Numero uno* to this day. Years later, on my fiftieth birthday, Terry surprised me with a savings passbook marked "Italy." He recorded the sum of $400 in the top column. My birthday card read: "This is a down payment for a return trip to Bellagio. Love, Terry."

"I figure if we put away a hundred or so each month, we can swing a return trip in about a year. That's if you can control your spending. Can you manage to limit your shopping for clothes and household doodads?" Terry asked.

"Of course. For a return trip to paradise, I'll try hard."

But I continued to spend.

He continued to drink.

DARK WINE WATERS

CHAPTER THREE

Life at Sea

They are not long, the days of wine and roses.

Ernest Dowson

After Europe, Terry spent most nights at my place, but sneaked out early, before Matt woke up. The lease on my rental cottage ran out. When that happened, I rented the top two floors of a cavernous three story house in the East End district near downtown Charleston. Two fun-loving bachelors rented the first floor. Although the house was a "fix 'er up" special, the location was ideal, with an elementary school one block away. On my $15,000 yearly salary plus child-support payments, I could easily handle the $250 a month rent.

My impending divorce led to a series of do-we or don't-we live together discussions for Terry and me. I don't recall who initiated the topic, but Terry and I volleyed that do-or-don't ball back and forth in heartfelt conversations at my kitchen table.

"So what do you think, Frannie? It kind of makes sense for us to live together since I'm practically living with you and Matt already."

"I'm not sure I'm ready to live with someone. And I'm concerned about Matt's reaction. Besides, you've never been around kids. You've never even been married. Matt adores you. But he misses his father. And two men in his life right now might be confusing."

"Matt's a special kid and we get along fine. And you know I won't interfere between Matt and his dad."

"I know, but this long distance parenting is complicated."

"Well, best I can tell, we're already living together. And anyway, Anthony is living with that woman. So he can't object."

Still bitter over the divorce, I shot back, "I don't give a damn whether he objects or not."

"Hey, calm down. Do you want a drink?" He poured scotch over a tall glass of ice.

"No thanks. I'll make some tea. I know you spend a large part of your time here but as long as you're paying rent on your apartment, we aren't living together."

"That's a technicality. If I spend all of my time with you here, does it make sense for me to pay rent every month for an apartment I don't live in?"

"Is that a rhetorical question?"

He moved forward, put his arm around my shoulder, raised his glass and grinned. "Cheers."

Our decision to "shack up," as Terry called it, felt as normal as wrapping myself in a bathrobe to retrieve the morning paper or swimming in a calm lake. That was one part of the equation. The other had to do with revenge. Matt's father, Anthony, had "shacked up" the very day that my son and I headed north on the West Virginia Turnpike in my Corolla station wagon. The thought of Anthony's girlfriend living in my house in Chapel

Hill, cooking in my kitchen, sleeping in my bed, having sex with my husband, and interacting with my son enraged me. Looking back, I realize that both Anthony and I should have put the brakes on cohabiting so soon after our separation. Blinded by both romance and anger, I placed my needs above my son's when he was most vulnerable.

Thankfully, Matt adjusted well. He loved his father, who visited often, and he bonded with Terry. Matt rarely played one against the other. Like plaintiff and defendant before a judge, Anthony and I restrained ourselves in our son's presence. In retrospect, I'm grateful that we pulled together on major decisions affecting Matt's life.

Money was tight, so I scoured thrift shops to decorate our apartment. I'd arrive early at estate sales and frequented secondhand furniture stores hunting for tables, chairs, bureaus, and desks. I'd recruit Terry to haul my treasures in a friend's orange Volkswagen camper. After work and during weekends, I enlisted Terry's help to strip, sand, stain, and paint. Like an artist contemplating a blank canvas, I pored over paint samples.

"What do you think of this yellow for the kitchen? Do you think it's too bright?" I asked as I flicked ashes into a glass green ashtray.

"You're better at that than I am. Whatever you decide is okay with me."

"Can't you simply give me a clue?"

He couldn't.

And he didn't.

During those first weeks, ladders, paint cans, and brushes littered the rooms. The apartment reeked of fresh paint and turpentine. The large rooms with high ceilings accommodated bright colors: royal blue, sunshine yellow, and new spring green. However, the deep purple enamel paint in a tiny half-bath was an unwise choice, which I never remedied. I stenciled white clouds over the baby blue ceiling in Matt's bedroom as lovingly as Michelangelo in the Sistine Chapel. Matt and I arranged his Matchbox cars, Fisher Price toys, blocks, puzzles, and his many Caldecott picture books on the shelves that filled one entire bedroom wall. Bright red beanbag chairs waited in front of a bay window for someone to sit in them.

Terry surprised Matt with a set of Dallas Cowboys sheets.

"Going to make a Cowboys fan out of that boy," Terry told me. (Matt, who eventually did become an avid Cowboys fan, unearthed those faded sheets when he packed up to leave for college.) While I read him bedtime stories and stroked his hair, Matt and his stuffed Snoopy cuddled with the Cowboys and drifted into that untroubled slumber of childhood.

After each room in the apartment glistened with fresh paint, we tackled more challenging tasks like hanging window shades. Brandishing his newly acquired power tools, Terry drilled holes to hang prints, posters, and plants.

Hanging a lamp, the kind that swung from a thick gold chain, was a two-person job. Terry climbed a ladder and drilled two holes in the ceiling: one in a corner of the room and another about three feet in front of it. With two hooks secured, we wrestled with the lamp's metal chain, which refused to climb the wall. After several tries, it looped in a graceful arc to support the lamp below. Terry climbed down the ladder.

"It's too low; someone's going to knock into it," I said.

"Not to worry. We're both short. Besides I don't want to fool with the damn thing again."

"Sorry, it won't do. We have to hang it higher."

"Let's take a break." He opened the fridge, downed a cold Budweiser, grabbed another and then climbed back up the ladder. Once again we tussled with the chain and positioned the lamp. It was still too low. But I let it go.

Our decorating continued at a fast pace. Shiny philodendron and thick asparagus ferns cascaded from macramé planters fastened to the ceiling with gold-colored hooks. We rolled olive green and gold shag carpets onto hardwood floors in our living and dining rooms. (How I managed to vacuum those carpets with the consistency of crab grass is a mystery.) A string of multicolored glass beads hung in the open kitchen doorway to add a Middle Eastern touch. Several then-ubiquitous prints and posters graced the walls: Robert Indiana's "Love" lithograph, the Casablanca movie poster of Bogie in a trench coat with a cigarette dangling from his mouth, and Van Gogh's Sunflowers. Terry purchased bricks and boards from a lumberyard and assembled bookshelves for our collection of hardcover and paperback books, including textbooks from college.

We floated calmly through those halcyon days of impromptu parties, potlucks, fondue feasts, food and babysitting co-ops, consciousness-raising groups, and new friends and acquaintances. Charleston is a cozy city with about three degrees of separation. Folks are friendly and newcomers welcomed. We socialized with other new faculty members from the college. I joined NOW (the National Organization for Women) and befriended fellow feminists, several of whom have remained close friends. Terry introduced me to his Texas buddies who'd migrated to the lush West Virginia hills because land was cheap. They teased me about my New York accent but welcomed me to their fold. "She's not so bad for a Yankee."

Because our apartment was large and centrally located in town, friends and their young children congregated there. When families arrived, the kids raced to Matt's bedroom on the third floor, where they built forts with cardboard boxes, sheets, and pillow cases, raced Matchbox cars, and constructed elaborate towers from Lincoln Logs and Legos. They'd surface for juice and snacks or to tattle on one another.

The adults smoked cigarettes, and drank beer and gallons of cheap Gallo red. A few stepped into the hallway to smoke a joint. As we munched on cheese, crackers, and potato chips, we shared stories about our lives before moving to "The Mountain State," compared notes on our kids, worried about the sorry state of local schools, puzzled over hillbilly neighbors with their funny accents and rustic ways, and chortled about corrupt politicians in Southern West Virginia. And Terry reviewed the latest movies.

A walking encyclopedia of film trivia, Terry relished nothing more than catching old black-and-white flicks on late night TV. Although he practiced law, Hollywood was in his heart. Too shy for acting, he could have become a screenwriter or director. In my younger years, I'd harbored similar dreams.

But like Terry, I'd chosen a safe, secure profession—in my case, teaching—over my dream of becoming a writer. Words have always been my strong suit. My Aunt Vivian recalls how at the tender age of eighteen-months, I could recite nursery rhymes word-for-word. Although reading wasn't featured in my childhood home, I discovered the local library early on. "That Frances, always with her nose in a book," my father would say. My mother, a first-generation Italian-American who grew up poor, couldn't understand. "Where do you get those ideas, Frances? A writer? How are you going to earn a living as a writer? Become a teacher like your cousin Barbara. She earns a good living and has summers off."

Both Terry and I had our noses in many books. With Matt in tow, we often visited the county library, which was located a block away from Terry's office. During that time, I consumed nonfiction: spirituality, Eastern religions, polemics by feminists like Gloria Steinem, and inspiration by authors like Leo Buscaglia. As a kid, I had been drawn to the lives of the saints and mystics like St. Teresa of Avila, who founded the "barefoot" Carmelites. I marveled at her unstinting faith, her devotion, and her sacrifice.

I still do. Back then, I had to redefine myself as a divorced, single parent, living with a significant other without the benefit of marriage. I turned to books to learn how to navigate in those uncharted waters.

While I sought enlightenment, Terry escaped, with spy novels and detective stories. A big fan of Louis L'Amour, he introduced me to that author, as well as to Dashiell Hammet and Frank Herbert. Books on cinema and old Hollywood film stars littered our living room.

One day Terry arrived home carrying a coffee-table biography of Charlie Chaplin illustrated with photos of his famous persona "The Tramp." As he sat at the kitchen table nursing a scotch and flipping through the pages, Terry asked: "Have you seen many of Chaplin's films?"

"Probably, but I don't remember much about them."

He looked at me as if I'd sprouted antlers.

"Say it ain't so, Frannie."

I shrugged. "What can I say? I don't remember."

"Come on, you're joshing me, aren't you?"

"Why would I do that?"

"Because Chaplin's one of the outstanding actors in film history. Guess I'll have to rent some of his films for you. Matt would like them too."

"Where are you going to get the movies?"

"I'm pretty sure they have them at the Library Commission."

And so it came to pass that Terry hosted a Chaplin film festival. Like a jury deliberating over a verdict, he pondered which films to screen.

"I'm definitely showing *The Gold Rush*. But I'm not sure whether to get the original or the later reissue."

"Is that the one where he eats his shoe?"

"Yeah, that scene's a classic."

A film purist, he opted for the original 1925 version of *The Gold Rush*. He objected to reissues, especially the colorized versions of black-and-white classics, like *It's a Wonderful Life*. "I can't understand why they mess around with those great movies."

Much thought was expended on selecting the second film for his double feature. "I'm leaning toward *The Kid*; it's sad and funny. I think the kids would like *The Kid*. Hey, that's funny. Kids, kid. Want a beer?"

I drink beer only with pizza, and even then I could settle for a Diet Coke. But for Terry, beer was ubiquitous. I can't recall a time when there wasn't a six pack of Bud in our fridge and a generous supply of Johnnie Walker in the liquor cabinet. He never ran out. I didn't give it much thought back then. Everyone smoked and drank, some more heavily than others. Perhaps I was already in denial.

The day before the screening, he lugged an eight millimeter projector, portable screen, and two reels of film up two flights of stairs and set them in our living room.

Word of the festival traveled fast. On a Saturday afternoon, some thirty adults and their offspring packed our living room. (The tall ones ducked under the still-too-low lamp.) I stocked Coke, apple juice, popcorn, and pretzels for the performance; members of the audience arrived with six packs of Bud, bottles of Gallo, guacamole, chips, and brownies. Fortified with drinks and snacks, the crowd settled down. Matt and his buddies occupied front row center. Terry set up the portable screen in the center of the room and struggled to thread the film through the projector's labyrinth of loops. I pulled the shades and dimmed the lights. When the sharp projector light hit the blank screen, the kids bounced up and giggled as their shadows danced in the background.

"Okay, let's settle down, guys," Terry chastised, but only mildly.

For the next hour, we were transported from that living room on Virginia Street to the Klondike of Alaska. The kids howled when The Lone Prospector with his derby, tattered suit, mustache, and cane waddled onto the scene. We all roared during the film's iconic scenes: the starving Tramp fastidiously eating his shoe, the prospectors' cabin teetering on the edge of the cliff, and the dance of the dinner rolls. Adults and kids alike read the title cards of the silent classic aloud together as they appeared onscreen, and "ooh-aahed" when The Tramp and his sweetheart kissed as the film faded out.

After a short intermission, The Tramp reappeared in *The Kid*.

Here, he rescues an abandoned newborn ("the kid"), and raises him on his own. (The kid's "disgraced" single mother had left him, in hopes he would be adopted by a kind married couple.) This 1920s plot turns when the boy's mother, who'd become wealthy, searches for and finds her abandoned son. In a melodramatic climax, she reclaims the boy, who clings tearfully to his beloved "father," The Tramp. At movie's end, father and son are reunited by a do-gooder at the mother's new mansion.

As the final reel spooled, the kids jumped up and imitated Chaplin's waddle, and the projectionist wiped a tear from his eyes.

A month or so after the festival, a different melodrama unfolded. Terry's parents, Rex and Zinna, planned to drive from Dallas to West Virginia "That's super. I'm eager to meet them and for Matt to get to know them. I'll make sure he's not scheduled to visit with his father that weekend."

Terry blunted my enthusiasm, running his hand over his hair in a gesture that spoke of discomfort.

"Well, there's a little problem." My antennae went up.

"What's that?"

"I haven't told them that we're living together. My parents aren't churchgoers, but my mom's Southern Baptist roots run deep. She won't approve. Her father was a jackleg preacher in rural Arkansas."

"You haven't told them! You're kidding, aren't you? What are you going to do about it? Move out during their visit?"

He walked over to the fridge for a beer. "I don't know."

"When are you going to tell them, Terry?"

"Not yet. I'm waiting for the right time."

"But they're leaving Dallas in three days."

"I'll tell them before they get here."

I let it go because I knew that Terry was nervous about the visit. He had a complicated relationship with his father. Because of Rex's alcoholism, Zinna had divorced him when Terry was two. He and his son didn't have much contact when Terry was growing up. Years later, when Rex had stopped drinking, he and Zinna remarried. Terry was twenty-one. He told me that he was relieved when they remarried, because as an only child, he wouldn't have to worry about taking care of Zinna.

For this visit, he reserved a room for them at the Heart of Town Hotel. I tackled housecleaning, prepared homemade spaghetti sauce and a tray of lasagna. Matt and I baked chocolate-chip cookies. The family artist, Matt crafted a cheerful "welcome" sign on poster board with an array of colorful Magic Markers. On the morning of Rex and Zinna's arrival, we hung it on the front door and tied balloons to the mailbox.

His parents called from Atlanta the night before their arrival. Last chance for Terry to warn them about our living situation, and I was sure he would take it. He looked thoughtful as he hung up.

"When will they get here? Should I have lunch or dinner ready?"

"They'll be here mid-day."

"Then I'll have snacks ready. Cheese and crackers. What do they like to drink?"

"No booze. Rex is on the wagon. Sweetened ice tea." Terry grabbed a Bud and paced around the kitchen.

"Frannie, sit down. I have to fess up. I didn't tell them."

"You didn't tell them? How could you not tell them? This is crazy. What if they come in here and march right out again? I'll be mortified."

"That isn't too likely. Let's hope for the best and see what happens."

Spoken like a true addict; had I but known. This was an example of the family dynamics of addiction. Rather than tell his parents the truth, Terry engaged in magical thinking. He avoided the topic. He pretended that it would disappear like morning fog over the mountains surrounding our home. During those years, I, too, would become caught in the undercurrent of deception. It would take many years and my own entry into recovery, before I learned how to be honest with myself and others.

But when Rex and Zinna arrived, Matt won their hearts when he erupted through our front door to greet his new "grandma and grandpa" as they emerged from their Oldsmobile. During the next three days, they raved about my lasagna and played with Matt. Rex amused him with card tricks and pumped him "high and higher" on a swing at a nearby park. He cheered as Matt maneuvered around the monkey bars and careened to the bottom of the sliding board. They treated him to hamburgers and fries at the McDonald's on Capitol Street. The highlight of the visit was a trip to Kids' Country Toys where they set Matt loose with a twenty dollar bill to "buy whatever you want." He chose a toy gun, a plastic tomahawk, and Matchbox cars to add to his fleet.

The minute Terry's parents headed out the front door to return to their hotel room, Terry poured Jack Daniels over ice and repeated the exercise several times before bedtime. While his parents didn't seem to judge me to be a harlot who had corrupted their son, I imagined that Zinna fretted over our "living in sin."

A year later, we visited Rex and Zinna in Dallas. Shortly after our plane took off from the Kanawha County Airport, Terry ordered a Bloody Mary "to take the edge off", a sure signal that he was anxious about the upcoming visit.

"So what's going to happen with our sleeping arrangements?" I asked.

"Hard to tell, but I'll wager my mom maneuvers so we sleep in separate rooms. The house has only two bedrooms. I'm not sure how you feel about it, but I'd appreciate it if you'd go along. My mom tends to pout if she doesn't get her way."

"Well, it doesn't make much sense since we are sleeping together, but it's her house. Besides she was especially nice to me during their visit to Charleston. Raved about my lasagna. Babysat with Matt. And she kept saying, 'bless your heart,' to me. Is that a Southern expression?"

"I don't know. My mom and aunt say it all the time."

"Well, anyway, my mother would have objected to our living arrangement too. Good Catholic, you know."

Terry patted my shoulder and signaled the stewardess for another drink.

"You want anything?"

"A Tab. Don't you think you'd better slow down?"

He ignored my question, stared out the cabin window and twisted a tissue in his right hand.

I didn't mention his drinking again because I sensed his unease as our flight edged closer to Dallas.

"I need to fortify myself. Besides, it's only a Bloody Mary. Tomato juice is extremely nutritious." He winked and raised his plastic cup. "Here's to you, Frannie. Bless your Yankee heart."

Before we left the plane, Terry stashed several tiny sample bottles of Jack Daniels into the ever-present satchel that he'd purchased in Europe years before, and where he always hid his booze.

When we arrived at the Blackwell's tiny bungalow on El Rito in the northwestern section of Dallas, Rex placed our luggage in Terry's old bedroom. So far, so good.

The four of us spent that first day visiting Terry's beloved Aunt Frieda who lived in the upscale village of Highland Park, a ten-minute drive but worlds apart from Terry's parents' modest neighborhood. This well-loved lady who'd helped raise my husband greeted us warmly, served sweetened ice tea, and shared childhood photos, including a few of Terry sporting his Davy Crockett cap. While paging through a photo album, I learned that his ancestors were part Chickasaw and Cherokee. Like many families who go back a few generations in Oklahoma, the Blackwell's ancestors included Native Americans.

Rex treated us to dinner at El Fenix, a family favorite restaurant, where we stuffed ourselves on chips, salsa, soft tacos, enchiladas, guacamole, sour cream, refried beans, and rice.

"Can't get Tex Mex food like this in West Virginia," Terry said as he sipped sweetened ice tea. I was tempted to order a margarita, but ordered a glass of unsweetened ice tea with lemon.

Right before bed, Zinna carried a pillow, sheets, and blanket to the living room couch and fixed it up. "Terry, you'll sleep here and Fran can have your old room." We complied. Nothing more was said.

On subsequent visits, our sleeping arrangement remained the same, Terry on the living room couch, me on the foldout bed in Terry's old bedroom, and Matt with his father back East. Zinna finally lifted the embargo in 1979 when we made our union official at a small wedding in Charleston on a late March afternoon that was sweet with the promise of spring. Unfortunately, Terry's parents couldn't join the celebration because Rex was recuperating from a massive heart attack. However, my father flew in from New York to give away the bride and babysit his grandson.

"Don't worry about a thing, you two. Matt and I will be fine," my dad said as we carried wedding gifts to my Toyota. After hugging Matt, we newlyweds headed south for a short honeymoon at Holden Beach with an overnight stop at Pipestem Resort.

On my first wedding night in 1964, I had lost my virginity. On my second, fifteen years later, I lost some of my naiveté. Since Terry drank too much and passed out, I didn't get to doll up in my new negligee or douse myself in Shalimar as I'd hoped to do. Instead, I read myself to sleep. Our wedding night wasn't anything like our romantic evenings in Paris.

The following morning, my new husband greeted me with a hot cup of coffee and a sheepish smile. "Frannie, I'm sorry about last night. I was exhausted when we left Charleston. Probably drank too much. Every time I turned around, someone was toasting. Best I can tell there wasn't a drop of champagne left from that case I ordered. And my allergies are kicking up. It's coming on that time of year. So how's my blushing bride this morning?"

"Fine, I guess," I answered flatly.

"So when do I get to see that sexy black nightie you told me about?" he winked.

This scenario became all too familiar in our relationship. The morning after a drinking episode, Terry would apologize with a joke, a kiss, and a peace offering. More times than not, in the beginning, I merely let it go.

Although wounded from the disaster of our honeymoon night, I chose not to drag out our melodrama. When Terry drank too much, he was genuinely sorry. Consequently, I forgave him. Was that love or denial? Probably both, but I didn't recognize my denial at the time.

"Why don't you buy me some breakfast?" I said.

"You got a deal."

After gorging ourselves at the breakfast buffet, we returned to our room and made love. After a quick shower, we packed the car and headed for a three-day honeymoon at Holden Beach in North Carolina, a place I'd become familiar with from prior trips with Matt and his father, and which I still loved.

"You'll love it there, Terry. Wait and see."

As we approached the Inter Coastal Waterway, the swing bridge parted to make way for a shrimp boat. When the ocean came into view, Terry squeezed my hand. We parked at the pier and ran to the water's edge. I dipped my hand into the foam and splashed him. "Wow. It's cold this time of year," he said as he reached over to tackle me.

After that rocky start, the rest of our honeymoon was sublime—lazy mornings of chilled champagne, late evenings of sumptuous sex, and afternoon excursions to Captain Pete's for the catch of the day. We took long walks along the shoreline in the low light of early evening toward an inlet on the west side of the island and enjoyed fresh fish and chilled white wine for dinner. We had soulful conversations as we glided back and forth on wooden rockers, bundled in heavy sweatshirts and listening to the ocean's heartbeat. Surrounded by starlight, we shared hopes and dreams for our future together.

"Look up, Frannie, see those stars. I think that's Leo the Lion. Kind of looks like a question mark. Can you see it?" Terry drank tumblers of scotch and puffed on cheap cigars. I wrapped my cold hands around mugs of hot tea. Once indoors, we made love, as waves locked in moonlight rolled onto the shore outside.

I could not have written a more perfect script or chosen a more perfect setting. We returned to Holden Beach many happy times after that, although none was happier than that idyllic honeymoon trip.

PART II

Muddy Water

THE ADDICT BECOMES ANXIOUS, DEPRESSED,

AND LACKING IN JOY. USE ESCALATES; DENIAL

INTENSIFIES. PROBLEMS, SUCH AS FREQUENT

CONFLICTS WITH FAMILY MEMBERS, APPEAR.

DARK WINE WATERS

CHAPTER FOUR

Troubled Waters

I am not afraid of storms for I am
learning how to sail my ship.

Louise May Alcott

For the next few years, we sailed on an even keel except for Terry's intermittent binges. Because they were infrequent and didn't interfere with our day-to-day routine, I tolerated them. My husband was never a nasty drunk, always contrite after each episode and always promising to cut down on his drinking. Back then I viewed each event as an isolated incident, like a faint ripple in a calm pond. The incident passed and wouldn't occur again. It rolled by like a passing wave. Here now, then gone.

Such is the power of denial.

Denial is a symptom of the disease. That's one reason addiction is so baffling and powerful. Addicts are masters of deceit. Their loved ones either comply or confront. Depending on my mood, I did one or the other. I hadn't yet learned how to do anything else.

Terry pulled his weight with household chores. Since I disliked grocery shopping, he pulled double duty at Kroger.

"Okay, Frannie, you make the list. I'll shop and unload, but you put away, and cook dinner tonight. How about meatballs? I love your meatballs."

Much time was devoted to work. Although careless about his appearance, Terry was devoted to his Legal Aid clients and meticulous about his legal briefs. When he worked at home, he'd often call out, "How do you spell . . .?" Then I'd slowly enunciate the letters in words like "mer-i-tor-i-ous," or "sub-stan-ti-al."

"How is it that you graduated from law school and can't spell?"

"I've heard tell that there's absolutely no relationship between spelling and intelligence, Frannie."

"Well, some of my students can't spell, and I'm not so sure how smart they are."

We attended Matt's parent-teacher conferences, helped with his homework, and reveled in his accomplishments, like his second-place win for a visual perception project in the county science fair, and ribbons for his art project. I swam laps at a local pool and hit Saturday morning yard sales. Once Terry signed up for a pottery class and presented me with a muddy brown, hand-built creation. A lopsided vase.

"Guess I'm no Michelangelo, but give me credit for trying." He played poker on Thursday evenings and hacked around the golf course with his buddies.

Some weekdays we'd play hooky to catch a new film release. Terry preferred matinees. "It's cheaper and less crowded." On weekends we often went to the movies with another couple, Jay and Mindy, whom we'd met shortly after arriving in Charleston, and who quickly became our close friends. Jay, an engineer at a leading chemical company, had a wicked sense of humor and could repair nearly anything. Mindy had the voice and flamboyant flair of Tallulah Bankhead. She loved cats and her garden. We met at the pool two nights each week to swim laps. At the movies, Terry and Jay favored macho dramas like *Platoon*. I recall Matt and Terry's excitement over the *Star Wars* trilogy, my copious tears during *Terms of Endearment*, and Terry's during the race scene in *Chariots of Fire*. He never missed a showing of *The Wizard of Oz*. His eyes misted when Judy Garland sang "Over the Rainbow." We never missed *It's a Wonderful Life* during the holiday season. Who couldn't love a guy with such a tender heart?

After an afternoon matinee, Jay, Mindy, Terry, and I often headed to Chili's in the Town Center Mall for nachos and chips, beer and margaritas. Sometimes, we drove to the Southern Kitchen, an ancient establishment with its army of ceramic chickens and roosters perched on shelves and a waiter who wore a hairnet. We settled into a booth on hard wooden benches. While Terry ordered chicken-fried steak; I favored home-style veggie soup. Jay ordered breakfast, which was served twenty-four hours a day. Mindy selected a medium-rare hamburger and fries. Sometimes we'd split an order of fried onion rings or splurge on blackberry cobbler topped with vanilla ice cream.

One night we headed to Jay and Mindy's for pizza and beer. Terry was restless and kept excusing himself to go outside. The Gino's pizza delivery guy arrived.

"Should I go outside to look for Terry?" I asked.

"He's probably in the bathroom. Let's dig in while it's hot," said Mindy. The three of us stuffed ourselves and then sipped beer and smoked cigarettes. After we polished off most of the pizza, Mindy leaned forward to light a Marlboro.

"Is Terry still in the bathroom?" I asked.

Jay sprang up. "I'll go look." He searched up- and downstairs and then grabbed a flashlight to survey the front yard, the back porch and woods behind. "Can't find him in or out," he reported back.

I looked out the kitchen window. "Our car's still in the driveway. He has to be somewhere around here."

"I'll take a look in the basement, but I can't imagine why on earth he'd go down there," Jay replied.

But there he was, passed out on the concrete floor at the bottom of the stairs. Jay lifted him, guided him up the stairs, and planted him in the bathroom. I ran a washcloth under cold water and wiped the blood from a cut on his forehead.

"Are you hurt? Do you need to go to a hospital?"

"No, no, I'm fine," he replied. A few minutes later, he joined us. "Damnedest thing. I heard Blackberry meowing and went to open a door to let her out. I thought she was stuck in a closet. Instead I must have opened the basement door. Seemed to have lost my footing and fell. I don't remember anything except Jay pulling me up. Where's the cat?"

"I think she's outside. Boy, were you lucky. You could have cracked your head open on that floor," Mindy observed. "Here." She handed him a plate and a slice of reheated pizza "Looks like you could use a good, stiff drink. What do you want?"

"A Coke with tons of ice. Or do you have any Tab?"

"You want some rum in it?"

"No, plain is fine."

The night that Terry fell down the basement stairs and didn't break his neck became a comic event in the annals of my husband's drinking escapades. After all, no permanent damage, no harm done. *Besides, who doesn't get tipsy once in a while?*

That wasn't the only time Terry fell. One snowy evening when Matt was in seventh grade, we attended a neighborhood party. Because the roads were icy, we decided to leave the car and walk home with Matt and a few of his friends. As we made our way down a steep hill, Terry fell forward and hit his head on a concrete stair step that was covered with ice. Blood gushed from his forehead and he couldn't get up. I tried to remain calm and asked Matt to run to the nearest house to telephone our friend, Barry, who'd hosted the party. Matt's friends raced behind him. A few minutes later Barry arrived, and with the boys eased Terry into Barry's car. We drove home in silence. I cleaned and bandaged Terry's wound and helped him to bed. The following morning, I approached Matt cautiously because I knew he had been embarrassed in front of his friends. He didn't want to talk about what happened. All he said was "Mom, I don't understand why he doesn't stop."

I didn't understand either. Back then I had no concept of addiction as a disease and kept making excuses when isolated drinking episodes occurred. During my recovery I came to understand that denial was a toxin. In my twelve-step program, I would be introduced to tools that would help me deal with the truth. But I didn't have them back then.

On the surface, our marriage appeared normal, in ways, even ideal. Terry shared his passion for the Dallas Cowboys with Matt and they caught all of the games on TV. Terry and I worked hard. I enjoyed teaching but didn't relish grading tons of student essays. Sometimes, Terry dragged his briefcase home to complete copious law briefs. On the weekends, we kicked back with takeout pizza and rented videos. We delighted in sitting on cushions in front of a blazing fire on cold winter nights listening to the sounds of The Beatles, The Moody Blues, and Keith Jarrett.

One Christmas, Terry struggled to set up a VCR, a surprise gift for the family. In years to come he watched scores of basketball and football games on tape and taped old movies and TV shows. *Dallas*, which ran for thirteen seasons, from 1978 to 1991, was a favorite. He didn't miss one episode, including the notorious "Who Shot JR?" cliffhanger. Not a big TV fan, I passed on *Dallas* and rarely watched the ball games, but I did get to see some of Terry's footage.

During one of my classes, I'd planned to show a video on contemporary poets. Instead of the beginning credits to the program, my students were treated to a scene featuring Little Joe and Hoss jawing on the Ponderosa. They had a good laugh, and I had to regroup to fill forty-five minutes of class time. (I still cannot bring myself to discard Terry's collection of videotapes, which includes Laurel and Hardy, Abbott and Costello, Fritz Lang's *Metropolis*, and a bevy of Hitchcock classics like *The 39 Steps* and *Secret Agent*. The tapes are stored in boxes in the garage where they collect dust.)

On long walks along the river or in Kanawha State Forest, we held hands as our beloved German Shepherd, Lucky, sniffed at the base of every tree. To celebrate each New Year, Jay and Mindy joined us for a walk in the forest, even when the temperature hovered in the teens. Back home, I'd serve a Smithfield ham, along with collard greens and black-eyed peas, using Zinna's recipe. According to Southern lore, if folks eat greens (to represent dollars) and peas (coins), they'll reap financial rewards during the coming year. To top off the meal, Mindy contributed the last of her holiday fruitcake, baked by her mother-in-law. "You'd better eat all of it. What's left goes in the trash."

"You make it sound mighty appetizing," Terry responded.

Every spring, I prepared the garden beds while Terry hauled heavy bags of mulch, manure, and top soil. "You're management, Frannie, and I'm labor," he'd tease as he struggled to dig a hole big enough to plant a weeping cherry or red bud tree. "That damn red clay. I need a sledgehammer to break it apart." He joked that my third husband would be Joe, the gardener, a big-mouthed, burly guy who owned a local nursery. "Think about that. You can get all the plants and mulch you want for free."

"What makes you think I'd ever marry again after you, Terry? You're a handful."

No matter the season, I swam laps at the Y. The pool was comforting: the clean odor of chlorine, the straight lines of lap lanes, the chill on first leaping into the water, the silence while gliding from one end to the other, and the feeling of accomplishment when finished. I could let go and surrender in the safe, familiar pool.

In early April, Terry would litter the dining room table with tax forms and cancelled checks. He never cheated, although he itemized liberally and joined the midnight throng at the downtown post office on April 15. And every autumn we'd rake and bundle bags of leaves from the hardwood trees surrounding our home, clean out muck trapped in gutters, and hose down and carry the patio furniture to the basement.

In winter we shoveled snow in the steep driveway leading up to our house. (Although Terry purchased an electric snow blower, it proved to be too unwieldy for the driveway.) During a storm, we'd stand by the French doors leading to the patio and watch cars slide down the hill in front of our house. If school was out and offices closed, we'd grab sleds buried in the basement and head to Coonskin Park with Matt.

One year we joined friends on a ski trip to Canaan Valley. Terry tackled the beginners' trails. After one lesson of frequent falls in bitter cold, I retreated to the cabin and settled in front of a roaring fire with a good book. That evening Terry drank too much and passed out after dinner. No one commented on his absence. I remember sitting at the edge of a bed crying while Mindy held my hand and consoled me. Early the next morning, I packed up our gear and made some excuse about why we had to leave early. We didn't speak as I drove home. For the next few days, I gave him the silent treatment, after which he promised to straighten up and cut down on his drinking. I believed he was sincere and forgave.

But his drinking progressed. I doubled my time in the swimming pool and added a short prayer that I'd learned from the nuns. With each lap, I'd silently repeat, "Lord have mercy." Breathe, stroke, pray. Breathe, stroke, pray. Back and forth, from one end of the pool to the other. If the pool was my church, then the ocean was my cathedral. Each year, Terry, Matt, and I looked forward to our weeklong vacation at Holden Beach with sharp anticipation.

We'd rent a beachfront house with Jay and Mindy, and over the years, we settled into a comfortable routine. Long walks to the point at the inlet, fresh fish at Captain Pete's, and trips to Beach Mart to purchase suntan lotion, rafts, film, and plastic buckets and shovels. Terry strolled to the pier late mornings to pick up several newspapers. I can see him on the deck shuffling the sports pages, sipping a Bloody Mary, and gazing at the ocean. Late afternoon we sipped cocktails on the deck, dipped taco chips into Terry's infamous dip of spicy Rotel sauce and Velveeta cheese, and fed the black grackles that hovered hopefully near the food.

One year, Terry was delighted when the house we rented had a large icemaker built into a bar. A Southern boy weaned on gallons of sweet ice tea, my husband craved ice. Loads of it. He was rarely without a drink in one of his Go-Mart plastic mugs filled to the brim with ice cubes and scotch, Tab, or sweetened tea. In later years, he switched from scotch to vodka to mask the smell of alcohol.

Usually laid back, at least on the surface, Terry was compulsive about three concerns: calling his mother in Dallas every Sunday, balancing our checkbook, and refilling ice cube trays. At least eight plastic trays were stashed in our freezer at all times, with extras stored in the pantry. When one cracked, he replaced it with a backup from the pantry. When one was put back into the fridge empty, he pouted. Often I tossed the empties in the drain board and failed to refill them or, worse yet, I'd wedge one in the back of the freezer with the tray only half full. "No offense, Frannie, but it's a simple enough thing to refill a tray." Although I tried, I never measured up to his exacting ice-tray standards.

The drinking continued and as time passed, I began to confront or try to reason with him. I recall long conversations late into the night. I talked; he listened and always promised to cut down. Sometimes he could handle a few drinks without getting drunk; other times he couldn't. His shift from social to problem drinker was gradual, like the slow rise of the sun over the horizon at Holden Beach. That's why I often viewed each binge as a temporary glitch. Like other spouses of alcoholics I spent too much time and energy trying to maintain the façade of a healthy, normal marriage.

Often in the aftermath of a drinking episode, I turned the thermostat up; he turned it down. He'd retreat and I'd sulk or, more often, let loose with tantrums, tears, and threats, particularly if powered by PMS.

"It's that time of month again. Frannie, I'd better watch out."

Once I threw a vase across the room. It shattered to pieces. We stood silent for a few minutes until he gathered up the shards in a dustpan. Another time, I clenched my fists and pummeled his chest: "Why are you doing this? Why won't you stop? Why won't you answer me?" Like a wave about to crest, my frustration mounted. A few times when Terry fell out of bed, I stepped over his inert body and left him on the floor. I lacked the compassion to at least cover him with a blanket.

Frost for a few days, then the thaw. A touch, a kiss, a hug, an "I'm sorry," a single rose in a bud vase, a sticky note left on the refrigerator, or a bag of chestnuts. Nothing but smooth sailing ahead. Then we recalibrated our thermostats to a comfortable emotional temperature.

Because Terry was kind, gentle, and considerate, I felt conflicted. *Everyone indulges. Nobody's perfect. He's been working hard. I'm overreacting. I'm irritable this time of the month. Besides, it doesn't happen that often. I worry too much. I'm too serious. I need to lighten up.* Back then my denial was substantial. But Terry's was as obdurate as a rock face on a mountain. No doubt it was rooted in his upbringing. While his mother couldn't control her husband's alcoholism, like me, she also coped by making excuses, covering up, and minimizing damage. Different as Zinna and I were in most respects, in our reactions to an alcoholic spouse, we were remarkably alike. We veered between trying to control and outright denial. Giving up control has been the most difficult part of my recovery. I have had to revisit Step One "We admitted that we were powerless . . ." countless times. Still do.

However, when the elephant lumbered into the middle of the room, Terry and I were both forced to "fess up," as he used to say. It happened in San Francisco in the early eighties. I'd received a grant from the Bay Area Writing Project to bring its training program to teachers in West Virginia. Not only was the grant a boost to my professional career, but an opportunity to visit San Francisco for the first time. Terry arranged to join me. On the final evening of our four-day visit, a staff member, Molly, invited us to dinner. During the taxi ride to her apartment, I held Terry's hand and gushed about the steep hills, the bridge, the bay, and the enchanting row houses. "Cities. I love cities. And this one is so charming with the Golden Gate Bridge and the bay. Water everywhere. I absolutely love it. You know it's my dream to live by the water."

"Frannie, you're so restless. Frankly, I have no desire to move to a city anytime soon. Besides Charleston has water. The Kanawha River runs right through it."

"Oh, that puny river doesn't count."

Molly greeted us warmly at the door of her street-level apartment. She introduced her husband, Peter, a pipe-smoking poet, tall and lanky, looking like the actor Jeremy Irons. Dominating the narrow living room was an exposed brick wall lined floor-to-ceiling with shelves filled with books and magazines. Large canvasses of black-and-white nudes hung from the stark white walls. Urban chic, exactly as I'd imagined: high ceilings with exposed wooden beams, darkly gleaming windows with views of the bay, and polished hardwood floors.

I'm sure Molly and Peter were gracious hosts, but I don't recall our conversation or what we ate, because I was preoccupied with Terry's drinking. He downed several tumblers of scotch-on-the-rocks before dinner, imported wine during the meal, and brandy after dinner. As the evening progressed, his speech slurred. He was barely able to follow the conversation. Molly and Peter exchanged telling glances, as if to say: "When the hell are these strangers going to leave?" I felt as if one of Terry's precious trays of ice cubes had been dumped into my stomach. I wanted to disappear into a nook in the urban chic bookcase or jump out one of those gleaming windows into the bay. I imagined Molly recounting her evening with the pitiful lush and his hapless wife from West Virginia. I prayed that we'd avoid a scene. When espresso was served, I downed my cup, looked at my watch and announced, "Lovely evening. But we must get going. We have a long flight ahead of us tomorrow."

"Yeah, best to get going," Terry slurred, agreeably. We were almost there. Only good-byes and thank you at the door to negotiate.

And then it happened.

When he tried to lift himself up from the couch, Terry grabbed a floor lamp to steady himself. But both he and the lamp crashed to the floor. I wanted to wrap the lamp cord around my husband's neck and choke the life out of him.

"Are you hurt?" Peter asked as he set aside his pipe and sprang to lift him. Molly rushed for ice to stop Terry's nosebleed. I rushed in, to control the damage, excuses pouring from my lips with the practiced speed of the mortified spouse.

"I'm so sorry. We've been speeding around in this fabulous city to take in all the sights . . . Neither one of us has gotten much sleep . . . And Terry's always plagued with allergies. In fact, he had an attack this morning. He sneezes like crazy, his nose bleeds. Guess everything's caught up with him. He'll be fine after he gets some sleep. I'd appreciate it if you would call us a cab to take us back to the hotel."

"We could drive you," Molly said unenthusiastically.

"Absolutely not. I wouldn't think of it. Call us a cab, please. We'll be fine."

She looked relieved. Or did I imagine it?

As Terry slumped on the sofa holding a cold washcloth to his nose, Peter cleared his throat.

"You know I've done the same thing every so often. I remember one time we were running around in Spain. Think it was Barcelona or maybe Madrid. No matter. All that sightseeing wears you out. Rich food and too many drinks. We were in a bar one afternoon, and I don't remember much except a frightful hangover. Felt like hell the next day."

What a kind response.

"Happens to all of us, doesn't it?" I said weakly, through gritted teeth. "Well, I'm sure Terry will be fine by tomorrow."

Neither Peter nor Molly could meet my eyes.

The minute hand of the clock seemed stuck in place, but its too-loud ticking counted out an embarrassing and otherwise silent eon until the cab arrived. Peter lifted Terry, and we positioned him between us, hoisting his arms over our shoulders. He dangled between us like a scarecrow propped on a pole, albeit a scarecrow clutching a fistful of bloody tissues to his streaming nose.

When we arrived at the hotel, I stormed ahead of Terry through the lobby, leaving him to follow me into the elevator, if he could. Each of us turned, and faced forward, our eyes glued straight ahead. When the doors parted, I bolted ahead, opened the door to our room and slammed it behind me. A few minutes later he fumbled with the door knob. I considered locking the door but didn't want someone to find him passed out on the carpet in front of it. So I pulled the door open and glared at him. He looked away, wobbled across the room, and crashed on top of the bed with his clothes on. I removed his shoes and glasses, covered him with the duvet, and picked up the blood-soaked tissues that had fallen to the floor. Unable to sleep, I read late into the night, chain smoked, and threw myself a pity party in which I mentally compared us to our married friends who didn't have to deal with our problem. *Why can't we be like them? Why doesn't he simply stop? Why do I have to put up with this?*

The next morning, as Terry emerged from the shower, I lashed into him, in my best drama-queen persona. I paced in front of the hotel window, with a plastic ashtray in my left hand and a Salem 100 in my right, my voice tight and shrill. "If you ever pull a stunt like that again, I'm leaving you. I was never so embarrassed in my life. How could you? How could you?" I stubbed my cigarette butt hard into the ashtray and glared at him.

He didn't answer.

For the remainder of the day, our hearts froze in bitter silence. Silence as we ate breakfast, silence as we packed our suitcases, silence as we rode to the airport, and silence as we boarded the plane home. Although the elephant had trampled into the room, Terry wouldn't acknowledge its presence. This drove me crazy. A tailwind of guilt, shame, and anger propelled us from West to East and fueled our marriage for several more years. Terry tried to control his use of alcohol, while I tried to monitor and manipulate him. We treaded water to keep afloat and settled into an illusory life of managing the unmanageable.

DARK WINE WATERS

CHAPTER FIVE

Rock Bottom

The wild sea roars and lashes the granite cliffs below.

Mary Howitt

After a storm broke, we'd sort through the emotional debris and carry on. Over the years, we tried marital counseling. I flirted with recovery meetings for family members and suggested a twelve-step fellowship to Terry. Neither of us followed through. Finally, the creek beds overflowed, and the full force of his addiction overwhelmed us.

In May of 1986, we again rented a summer house together with Jay and Mindy. When our Chevy Caprice topped the bridge over the Intercoastal Waterway, Terry, Matt, and I cheered at the first sighting of the Atlantic, like sailors spotting land after a long stretch at sea. We settled into our comfortable beach routine. Terry floating beyond the breakers and surfacing on his silver raft to catch waves to the shore, or reading a Louis L'Amour or Dick Francis paperback, or sitting on a porch rocker and gazing at the horizon. A comforting quiet. At low tide we played a variation of *bocce* and scampered to catch the red and black balls before they disappeared into the sea. Matt, who was now sixteen years old, borrowed the car to drive to the pier where he played pool and hung out with other teens.

Late afternoons we raced to Captain Pete's for the catch of the day. Pete's was divided into two sections: the souvenir half housed bins of polished seashells, racks of suntan oil and cheap sunglasses, beach towels and mugs, hats, plastic jewelry, shovels, pails, whoopee cushions, rafts, tubes, and floats. The main, smaller, food section was crammed with bait, tackle boxes, bins of lemons, potatoes, and onions, Tabasco and Old Bay seasoning, cornmeal, peanuts, and Nabs, and a cooler filled with lemons, soft drinks, and bags of ice. One year the ruddy-faced, red-haired Captain himself shared his grouper recipe (top the fish with oil, tomatoes, green pepper, and onions and bake for an hour). "Pete's grouper," named for the Captain, became a vacation staple. When I decided to make scampi, Terry volunteered to peel several pounds of shrimp. "You got a deal, Frannie. If you cook them and clean up."

After dinner we spotted sand crabs with flashlights or scanned the star-streaked sky. "That's the Big Dipper. Some folks call it the Great Bear. Can you see it?" Sometimes we crouched behind the dunes to set off firecrackers. Late evenings it was backgammon, Scrabble (I usually won), poker, or old movies. Matt, who was the family visual artist, was a whiz at complicated puzzles. Last to bed, Terry lingered on the deck, nursing a scotch and puffing a cheap cigar. He wasn't a smoker, but a beach vacation afforded certain indulgences. Afternoons we made love to the sound of waves rolling toward the shore.

Jay and Mindy were outstanding housemates. Like high school cheerleaders, they wore us out with their energy and enthusiasm. They cooked gourmet meals and drank tons of beer. Late afternoons we gathered on the deck for cocktails. We snapped pictures and admired the view. We compared suntans and debated the merits of 15, 30, or 45 SPFs. "Didn't I tell you? You should have used the 45, not the 15; that's no protection at all." And we talked about the weather. "Paper says a 60 percent chance of rain tomorrow."

"No way. Look at that sky. Those weather forecasters never get it right."

As the sun tucked itself into the horizon, we sipped vodka collins or gin-and-tonics and savored Terry's famous Tex Mex dip, that culinary special of Rotel and Velveeta. We scooped it up with salty tostados and tossed crumbs to the grackles flying overhead.

Although Terry drank steadily during the week, he didn't appear to lose control. He downed a few beers during the day, a glass or two of wine at dinner, and nursed a tumbler of cognac late evenings as he sat on the deck and gazed at the stars. I noticed that his eyes were bloodshot but attributed it to the salt water. Once he wobbled a few times while carrying a float down the steps leading to the dunes.

"Is everything okay? You're a little unsteady on your feet."

"Guess that allergy pill got to me last night."

I know now that addicts engage in patterned, ritualistic acts. Terry was no exception. He always drank from a plastic mug, the kind you purchase at Go Mart. His mugs were always super-sized and always opaque, never clear.

From morning to night, he poured vats of Diet Coke or Dr. Pepper (never coffee) into his mug. He often laced his soft drinks with vodka or gin, which he must have thought would smell less like the liquor they were. Like a toddler clutching his teddy bear, he carried his mug from room to room: the kitchen, the bedroom, the dining and living rooms. He rarely left home without it.

Once I inadvertently picked up his mug from the kitchen counter and took a sip. When I tasted vodka laced with Diet Coke, I ran to find him.

"Terry, come here and taste this." Like a guilty child, he followed. "What's this?" I barked. "I thought you said that you'd cut down. Jesus Christ, it's eleven o'clock in the morning." He looked down, didn't respond, and walked away. Later, he apologized.

"I'm going to limit myself to one drink a day. I know that sometimes I drink too much, especially when I'm tired and stressed out. I said I'd cut back and I mean it. I promise."

There's no doubt in my mind that his promise was sincere, as was his belief that he could control his drinking. At that point, I tried to believe him, even though I suspected that he sneaked booze into the white plastic mug that he carried from room to room. Denial is the hub of the addiction wheel; it drives every spoke of the disease.

During the early 1980s, I traveled to teach courses and workshops in different southern West Virginia county school systems. Usually I spent one week away from home each month. This arrangement worked well for Terry. A solitary drinker, he could imbibe without any interference from me.

We kept afloat this way for several years, but the undercurrent of lies, anger, guilt, denial, remorse, and broken promises built up. It crested during another annual vacation at Holden Beach. Although Terry imbibed all week, my booze detector didn't register trouble signs. On the morning of our departure, I drove Matt to the beach house of a friend who'd offered to drive him to Chapel Hill to spend a week with his father. Then I returned to our vacation rental and began to pack for home. But I couldn't find Terry. Everyone else scurried, as if preparing for a hurricane: deflate rafts, hose-off decks, rearrange rockers, gather shells, clean out fridge, and pack up towels, swim suits, games, kites, booze, and leftover food.

"Do you want to save this cream cheese?" Mindy asked.

"Toss it and throw out those overripe peaches," I answered.

Mindy grabbed a half gallon vodka bottle from the freezer. "Gee, I thought there was more in this bottle. Oh, well, I'll stick it in the cooler with the other drinks."

"Looks like the fridge is empty. Give me some paper towels and I'll wipe it down," I said.

"Where's Terry?" Mindy asked. "Did he go out to get the paper or pick something up at the store?"

Where in hell is he? I wondered. I carried boxes and suitcases into the living room, my stomach tightening as I asked myself that question. I returned to the kitchen and then wiped down the fridge and collected trash bags to toss in the dumpster.

Mindy and Jay stuck around waiting for Terry to return. Their car was packed and they were ready to hit the road for the ten-hour journey home.

"Why don't you go on? He'll be back soon and he can help me carry stuff to the car."

"You sure? We'd be happy to wait with you. Besides, what if something happened to him?"

"Not likely. He probably decided to take a long walk. You know how he disappears sometimes." *Was it my imagination or did I see them exchange a "look"?*

"Go on, go, no use waiting. It's a long drive."

"Are you sure?

"Yes, go on."

"All right then, we'll see you back home. Call us when you get in."

They grabbed two garbage bags and left.

A half hour later, Terry returned, stinking drunk. Not slightly tipsy. He was stinking drunk: slurred speech, unsteady gait, and bloodshot eyes. Snockered, sloshed, smashed, shit-faced. *Thank God, Matt's gone and on his way to Chapel Hill.*

Although furious, I kept my mouth shut. In stony silence, we gathered our suitcases and bags. Terry tried to load the car.

Without making eye contact, I brushed him aside and flung suitcases into the trunk. Somehow he managed to position himself in the passenger seat. I revved the engine and headed for the dumpster where Terry tried to toss two garbage bags into the bin but missed and stumbled. At five-foot-two I strained to push the bags into the top of the dumpster and contemplated shoving Terry in as well. With this final chore complete, I slid back into the driver's seat, drove toward the toll bridge, filled up at the gas station, and headed home for the mountains.

Remarkably, during that ten-hour journey, I remained silent, setting an all-time record in restraint. Usually I raged; my weapon was words, my husband's was silence. I attacked; he dug in. The car reeked of cigarette smoke and anger as I drove along a two-lane blacktop bordered by scrubby pines and fields of soy beans and tobacco. We passed Shallotte and Whiteville. Outside Lumberton, I braked when Terry opened the passenger door to vomit. I pulled a musty beach towel from the trunk to wipe the door and headed north toward I-85 and Greensboro, then to I-40 and Winston-Salem. Slightly beyond King Tobacco (only in North Carolina would a town bear that name), I stopped in Mount Airy to grab a fast-food burger and fries, and get more gas. Terry remained in the car, still unconscious. Fueled by fury, I pushed past Pilot Mountain and hit the headlights at the tunnel on I-77. Shortly after that, the "Wild and Wonderful" sign appeared welcoming us to West Virginia.

During that memorable trip, I plotted various methods to murder my husband, like a hit man in *The Godfather*, one of Terry's favorite movies. Coppola's movie graphically demonstrates that sometimes blood is not thicker than water, as when Michael arranges to have his brother, Fredo, shot in a rowboat and dumped overboard into Lake Tahoe.

With neither lake nor rowboat, and with limited weapons available in the car, my options were few: grab a pillow from the back seat and smother him, or shove him out the passenger door, or wrap a kite string around his thick neck and hang him from a scrub pine. Ditching the car in a vacant garage with the engine running didn't seem practical. Besides, I couldn't pull it off. Tobacco sheds and trailers dotted the roadside, with few houses and no garages in sight.

At 9:00 p.m., we arrived in Charleston. Too exhausted to unpack the car, I eased Terry up the garage stairs and through the hallway to our bedroom where we both collapsed.

The next morning, fortified with my third cup of coffee, I sprang to full alert. I contacted Mary, a counselor friend.

"The situation with Terry at the beach last week was exceptionally bad. I need help. In fact, I'm desperate. I've got to arrange an intervention; he needs treatment immediately. Can you recommend someone who we can see in the next day or two?" Mary gave me several names and numbers. I soon located one who was available and set up an appointment for the following morning. Unfortunately, because of poor timing and lack of knowledge on my part, I failed to include close friends, including Mindy and Jay. So it would be one-on-one, not the best arrangement for an intervention.

When Terry woke up, I issued yet another in a long series of ultimatums. Only this time, I followed through.

"Either you go with me tomorrow and get treatment or I'm leaving."

It was as simple and as complicated as that.

No doubt experts speculate on the relationship between the rate of recovery for those who hit rock bottom and seek treatment of their own volition versus those coerced by family, employers, or a court order. However, one fact is unequivocal: only a crisis leads to intervention. The morning after we arrived home, Terry was quiet. Uncharacteristically he didn't try to minimize his behavior, although he hedged.

"I need to get back to work. I have a big court case coming up, barely enough time to complete a brief. I promise I'll go to the therapist once I get this brief out of the way. Look, I admit I have a problem and need help."

I held my ground. "It's either today, or it's over. I repeat: we deal, or it's over."

Unlike a few marital counseling sessions in the past, this wouldn't be the usual jawing about Terry's drinking and my codependence. This was different. I'd upped the ante, the stakes were higher, and a loss could wipe us out.

Since we arrived early, I flipped through a copy of *Newsweek* as Terry paced. After we filled out forms, the therapist introduced himself and ushered us into his office. Terry fingered a tissue as he chose a hardback chair adjacent to the counselor's metal desk. I sat opposite him. We began. Our warm–but-no-nonsense counselor steered me away from blaming and accusations.

"Fran, only the facts: specific events, times, people, and places. What did he do and how did it make you feel? Try this, 'Terry, when you . . . I feel . . .'" Experts recommend that the chief evidence be tied directly into the drinking whenever possible. No problem; I had plenty of specifics.

"Do you remember when you passed out on Sunday as we drove back from Holden Beach? I felt furious. Do you remember vomiting on the side of the road? I felt disgust. I had to drive ten hours by myself. I was exhausted when we arrived home. Do you remember last winter's ski trip to Canaan Valley; I think it was Presidents' Day weekend or something. We rented a cabin with Mindy and Jay and flipped a coin for bedrooms. We drew the loft. You fell out of the bed and spent the night sprawled on a cold floor. I went downstairs, sat in front of the fireplace and cried. Mindy made a pot of tea and sat with me. The next morning I made up some excuse so we could leave early. I felt ashamed and embarrassed. And how about that last visit to your family for Thanksgiving and how we almost missed our flight home because you spent so much time in the men's room? Or last Christmas when we missed a potluck because you were hung over? Holidays, that's your favorite time to mess up." On a roll, I barked out times and places and dates, like a deranged drill sergeant.

Several times the therapist interrupted to remind me to point out that this session was designed to help, not harm or judge or accuse. Embarrassed and ashamed, I cried as I remembered the countless events, times, and places when my husband had showed me his love. When he threw me a surprise party for my fortieth birthday, when he left Post-It love notes and sentimental cartoons on the fridge, when he cooked breakfast on Sundays, or massaged my feet. "Hey, it's going to be okay; come here and I'll massage your tootsies." Often when I taught evening classes and arrived home late, he ordered take-out Chinese: wonton soup and shrimp with lobster sauce, my favorites. He listened to complaints about my students' lousy term papers. "Frannie, they're eighteen, their hormones are raging, give them a break. You're an impressive teacher; they're damn lucky to have you."

I didn't recount his gentle and understanding way with Matt, who adored his stepfather. I didn't tell how Terry had asked my dad for my hand in marriage during one of our vacations at Holden Beach. Or how, on the night my father died, he held me until dawn and later brushed away my tears when Daddy's coffin was lowered into the grave at Calvary Cemetery.

My husband was a tender soul with a broken body and split personality. And therein lay my ambivalence and confusion. For years, I teetered on a tightrope between love and hate, rode a wave between drunk and sober, and fought a battle between blame and forgiveness. I became a "type"—a classic codependent.

Could this intervention tip the scale toward a normal, healthy relationship? Or was it too late?

Terry twisted the corner of his tissue and looked away from me. I grabbed a Kleenex to wipe my tears.

The therapist leaned forward. "Terry, do you admit you have a problem with drinking?"

"Yes."

"Are you willing to get some help?"

"Yes."

"That's good. There are many good programs available. Unfortunately, there aren't any inpatient treatment centers here. But there's one in Charlotte, North Carolina. I called this morning. They have an opening and can take you tomorrow."

Startled, Terry clutched his fingers around the bits of torn tissue and shifted in his chair.

Silence.

He regrouped and spoke in his soft voice. "Look. I admit I have a problem, but I don't need an inpatient facility. I don't want to leave. I have work to do, an important trial coming up. I can do outpatient here. I promise to comply with whatever you come up with."

The counselor looked at me. I shook my head. "No."

We played another hand. A skilled lawyer, Terry argued for outpatient.

"I can't pick up and leave today. I have too much work to do. Besides, I'll feel more comfortable handling this at home. I can get the treatment and still get some work done. I don't want to be away from my home, locked up in God-knows-where with a group of strangers."

I wasn't buying it; I refused to fold. In retrospect, that was a bad call. Terry didn't need to be stripped of his dignity in this potentially humiliating situation. He needed to have a say about his own treatment. This was his disease, not mine.

Then again, I had threatened to leave him before. This time I was determined to follow through. I knew that if he remained at home, he'd dance around outpatient treatment, one foot in tune with the program and the other out the door.

I bet that the therapist would substitute as "bad cop" for me. Not fair, but I didn't give a damn. Was it fair that my husband was an alcoholic? Was it fair that our marriage was strained and we were exhausted? Was it fair that Terry refused to stop drinking? Or thought he could control it? Was it fair that our lives were bookended by despair and hope? That denial had become the theme that ran through our relationship? That Terry wallowed in guilt and shame and I in self-pity and anger?

In the past, Terry ignored my threats because I'd failed to follow through. But this was different. *If I play my cards right and don't back down, he'll agree to go to Charlotte.*

How foolish those thoughts seem now. But in those days, I thought I was in control. I thought I could fix my husband. I wouldn't let go.

Finally, he folded.

"Okay, I'll go." His shoulders drooped. "Looks like I don't have any choice. Are you happy now?"

I hugged him. Of course I was happy. I thought our troubles were almost over. Still, we drove home in silence.

My husband, who loved to gamble, had often said, "Never wager more than you can afford to lose." Well, I thought I'd won this hand.

DARK WINE WATERS

CHAPTER SIX

Surfacing

If we do not change direction,
we are likely to end up where we are headed.

Chinese proverb

The night before he left, Terry packed his Lands' End duffel with three pairs of jeans, several long-sleeved cotton shirts, a windbreaker, underwear, socks, and a few paperbacks. I added a box of tissues, family photos from beach vacations, and a holy card sent to family and friends after my dad's death in 1980. The Prayer to St. Francis was printed on the back of the card. "Lord, make me an instrument of thy peace . . ." Terry packed his yellow Datsun and headed back South, less than a week after we'd returned from Holden Beach.

Usually medical insurance covers twenty-eight days of inpatient treatment. Although amenities differ, with the wealthy staying at private treatment centers with famous names and the indigent at state-run facilities, the protocol is the same. Upon arrival, clients are checked for alcohol and narcotics. Many detox for a few days before they settle into furnished, dorm-like rooms. The daily regimen is outlined, and rules are explained and strictly enforced. Counselors, including people in recovery themselves, are assigned. During the first week, visits aren't permitted and phone calls are limited. The daily program is packed with lectures, small-group and individual counseling sessions, twelve-step meetings, and time for reflection. Usually, family members participate during the second half of the program.

At the end of his first week, Terry contacted me. Our conversation was short because other patients were lined up at the one pay phone available.

"Good to hear your voice. How's it going?" I said.

"It's pretty regimented, but that's what I expected. They get us up early and we have talks and lectures in the morning, then a break for lunch. In the afternoon we go to group meetings. I've met privately with a counselor, twice. Guy's named Randy. I like him. In the evenings, they take us to twelve-step meetings. The staff is pretty nice. So it's not so bad. They have strict rules about the telephone, so I won't be able to call you too much. In fact, I need to get off soon because there's a line behind me waiting to use the one phone in the common area. Everyone smokes, it's killing me. How's Lucky? I miss her."

"Don't you miss me, too?" I asked.

"Don't be silly. Of course, I miss you. Oh yeah, I forgot to mention, the food is terrible, overcooked vegetables and Jell-O desserts, that sort of thing. There's a salad bar, so I'm not starving. Well, I'd better go. Talk to you later this week."

He rang off, and I stood there, looking at the phone and feeling strangely as if I hadn't spoken to my husband at all. More like a cheerful stranger stuck in a strange land where the food isn't to his liking, the people smoke too much, and oh, yeah, he misses his dog. No mention of the serious problem he was there to address. No asking how I was holding up. It was all about him.

Of course, I see that now, through the eyes of my own recovery. Back then, it was all too new.

Each client at the center received a treatment journal with topic headings ranging from "Daily Habits of Balanced Living," to "Self Image," to the "Physical Aspects of the Disease," to "Character Defects," to "Defiance."

Apparently "Defiance" resonated with Terry, because his July 7, 1986 entry appeared in bold, heavy strokes slanted sideways down the entire page, as if he were carving his words into the paper. Asterisks punctuate several entries like handwritten shouts. He wrote this:

> *Passive defiance, expressed indirectly, pouts, rationalizes, etc. denies true feelings, plays games, pretends to be all together, but really is being dishonest to self, procrastinates, puts things off, intellectualizes, pretends that getting well is like playing a game of cards, which card game do you get into if the stakes are your life?

In another section he wrote:

> **Beware of my ego! Remember the price I have to pay to drink. I'm an addict and I hate the people who tell me the truth and resent those who can drink. I have to be honest about this.

After a binge, Terry denied that he'd been drinking, even when he'd fallen out of bed or passed out on the recliner. He'd rationalize, minimize, and invent excuses. That drove me crazy. When I'd erupt into a storm of righteousness by pointing out that I had indeed found him lying on the bedroom floor, he'd calmly counter that I overreacted. "Frannie, you're making a big deal out of this. Lighten up." He never yelled or argued. Instead, he burrowed into the bunker of denial. He never accused me of causing him to drink. I never heard, "If it weren't for your nagging,

I wouldn't drink so much." Rather he'd say, "I'm genuinely sorry. I promise to try harder."

Months would pass without a drinking incident, which contributed to the crazy-making. When Terry brooded or suffered from a hangover, I blamed it on stress, fatigue, or his severe allergies. Although the verdant hills of West Virginia are magnificent, it's no place for folks who are allergic to pollen, ragweed, or mold. Because the line between a hangover and genuine allergy attack was blurred, I was often uncertain. This subterfuge fueled the insanity. I failed to connect the addiction dots because, for the most part, I refused to admit that I was powerless to make him stop drinking.

Addiction is a family disease; that's why family members are encouraged to participate in their loved one's recovery. I made the pilgrimage to North Carolina during the fourth week of Terry's treatment. Husbands, wives, moms, dads, siblings, and children of addicts gathered to learn about the disease and help their loved ones. We were free to unburden ourselves without apologies or embarrassment. No one judged us. We clung to each other like drowning victims and clung to the promise of recovery.

Although the characters and settings of the stories of addicts and their loved one differed, the plot was the same. Denial, dishonesty, and manipulation. Hope and despair; faith and fear. Some addicts were forced into treatment by the courts or employers. Some sought treatment on their own. Most had hit rock bottom, some more than once. Meanwhile, loved ones try to limit the damage. Our tactics don't work, but that doesn't stop us.

One afternoon our group leader asked for volunteers for a psychodrama session in which we'd play different roles of family members coping with addiction. The leader explained that the roles were based on the family systems' counseling model. The chief enabler, for example, covers up and makes excuses for the alcoholic so that he doesn't suffer consequences. A wife may call her husband's office to say he'll be late for work or cancel an invitation to a dinner party with some bogus excuse. The family hero compensates for the family's shortcomings. He gets straight As, edits the school newspaper, captains the swim team, holds down two part-time jobs, and tutors disadvantaged kids in his spare time. The hero excels. In contrast, the scapegoat is a family doormat who shoulders the alcoholic's blame. "If I weren't such a screw up, my dad wouldn't have to drink." And the mascot, or cheerleader, rallies family members when crises occur. Amid all the turmoil, the lost child, like Terry, retreats or disappears altogether. If any member decides not to play his or her role, then the system falls apart.

Our role-play scenario involved a wife confronting her husband about his drinking. I volunteered and slipped into my role easily. I began calmly, but soon the dialogue heated up. Like a blast of thunder before a storm, I let loose in a room full of total strangers.

"Why can't you stop? See how you're hurting yourself and your family. Don't you care what you've done to us? I've lost all respect for you and for myself. I've had it up to here. I'm fed up. I'm disgusted. I hate living like this." I shouted, I paced, I vented. "God damn it. Can't you see that you're killing yourself and wrecking our lives?"

I don't recall my "spouse's" response while I hammered at him. Maybe he was overwhelmed by my performance. Or, like Terry, he shut down. When the simulation ended, I rushed to the bathroom and vomited. As I wiped my face, I indulged in a short "pity party." *Why me? What the hell am I doing here? What have I done to deserve this?* Self-pity is as seductive to enablers as booze is to drunks. I dabbed my eyes with a tissue, sucked in air, and headed back to the group for debriefing.

Again and again during that week, I was forced to confront my poisonous behavior, to swallow my pride, abandon control, stifle self-pity, and focus on my own problems. I came to realize that I was as sick as my husband—two casualties afloat in the swamp of this family disease.

During family week, husbands, wives, daughters, sons, mothers, fathers, and siblings listened to lectures, shared stories, prayed, cried, laughed, reassured and bolstered one another, memorized slogans, and quoted from various recovery texts. Terry and I talked for hours over gallons of sweetened ice tea, and fed fat ducks as we circled a small pond in the sweltering Carolina heat.

Like a cool mountain stream, the twelve-step program soothed us with serenity and slogans. "Easy does it," "Let it begin with me," "Take what you like and leave the rest," "One day at a time," "Progress not perfection," and "Live and let live."

"Let go and let God" resonated with everyone. Since every cell of my body had been programmed to control, it seemed impossible to abandon my pride and tame my ego. Back then "powerless" wasn't part of my vocabulary. Although I'd been raised Catholic, my faith was fragile. Terry had long abandoned his Southern Baptist upbringing. We rarely attended church. At that point, I trusted my higher power about as much as I trusted my husband. However, I remained cautiously optimistic.

During one of our heart-to-heart conversations, Terry appeared to waver.

"I'm having some problems with parts of the program," he said.

"Like what?"

"It's not any one thing. The slogans and steps all make sense, but sometimes it feels like indoctrination. They keep slamming at it all the time."

"Well, from what I've heard, you can't let your guard down for a minute. You have to make recovery your number one priority. That's probably why the program has all these slogans and steps. They seem to have worked for the people who have successfully completed the program and now work here. You've heard the stories. Some are incredible. Peoples' kids banging on their bedroom doors while they're snorting coke, addicts sleeping on porches in the dead of winter, living in homeless shelters, bounced checks, bankruptcy, jail time, and God knows what else. I can't believe it. When I heard the stories, I thanked God we haven't had to go through that. They keep saying that you have to work the program. 'It works when you work it.'"

"Yeah, another slogan. Guess it's easier to 'talk the talk than walk the walk,'" he replied.

"Change is hard. That's why you're here for a month. That's why I'm here too. If it were easy, we wouldn't be here. Right?"

"Yeah, I guess so."

The climax of family week was our co-joint session, an hour-and-a-half debriefing with a counselor. Terry and I prepared for it by answering a series of questions beforehand. I remember how we sat on metal chairs in the middle of a dimly lit room and faced one another. I remember how we spoke softly. I remember how we held hands and cried.

This is what Terry wrote in his journal to share during our session:

1. *What do you like about your relationship?*

   Our love, sharing, and communication, how we supplement and support each other, walks, sex.

2. *What do you dislike about your relationship?*

   Style of our communication small irritations, decision-making, independence-dependence, Frannie's too serious, uptight, need more humor.

3. *What do you need?*

   Space and quiet time, stroking and acknowledgment and appreciation, expression of love.

4. What can you do to change your relationship?

Like myself and accept love; compromise, be open to change, express my feelings more, stop being passive defiant (pout, rationalize), not deny feelings, be honest (not lie), lower expectations of me and others.

5. What can your partner do to change it?

Listen, don't do ten things at once, don't make me guilty over her compulsiveness, prioritize, communicate differently, be less selfish, think before she says what's on her mind, when something happens to her she should get to the point, don't kill my interest.

6. What is stressful about your relationship?

My drinking, Frannie's reaction to it, finances, different priorities, different personalities, some differences in child rearing.

7. What do you want for the future?

Happiness and harmony and trust and security.

8. What are you willing to do for your recovery?

Try hard in the best way possible, give it priority.

I wasn't surprised by Terry's responses. We loved one another; our relationship was passionate. We both wanted happiness and harmony. I knew that his disease shamed him. I knew he hurt because I minimized his attempts to control his drinking.

"You don't give me credit, Frannie. You never stroke me for trying." I had no doubt that my romantic husband craved unconditional love. But unlike Terry's mother, Zinna, I could not love him unconditionally. She thought he was perfect.

Who am I to quibble with Terry's list of my character flaws? After all, he knew me better than anyone else. Nevertheless, that ice cube in my stomach surfaced as he read his responses at our co-joint session. It's humbling to be described as uptight, humorless, controlling, scattered, selfish, and irritating. I acknowledge uptight. I worry excessively. "You take yourself too seriously," Terry often said. Perhaps he considered me humorless because I can't remember jokes. Though I'm not the life of the party, I'm not a sourpuss either.

I also admit to "scattered." In one of my housecleaning frenzies, I had inadvertently thrown out a paycheck. Later, Terry rifled through garbage soaked with coffee grinds and rancid fruit to retrieve it. "Why do you have to do ten things at once?" he asked as his hand slid into the slime. Terry also was right-on about compulsive. On a scale of one to ten, I'm a nine. My husband's "It can wait until tomorrow style," was more a two or a one-point-five. He paid our bills in a timely fashion but didn't write a check the actual day one arrived in the mail. As for my irritating habit of shooting off my mouth without thinking first, I pleaded guilty. The slogan "Think" was not part of my vocabulary. Since I'd not yet learned to "Let go and let God," control proved to be a monumental hurdle. At the end of the session, the counselor suggested that we make a list of what we liked and disliked about one another. Perhaps I misunderstood, or perhaps our counselor was expecting too much of us. Whatever the reason, Terry and I were scarcely getting accustomed to the shallow end of the recovery pool, and this was like being thrown into the surf and asked to ride a forty-foot wave. However, we tried to comply.

I regret that I didn't keep a copy of my list from that session, but I recall most of it. Terry and I concurred on what we liked about our relationship: our love and support for one another. Many days we danced in harmony, sometimes whirling in pure delight. But intermittent binges wrenched our rhythm and crushed our spirits. The tide was either up or down in minutes, hours, or days. The line between our extremes stretched tight.

What I believed I most needed was for Terry to stop drinking, permanently. As for changes, patience was paramount on my list, followed by relinquishing my temper, cultivating compassion, and seeing a glass half-full instead of half-empty or, worse yet, shattered. Letting go and minding my own business were essential for my recovery. Like Terry, I longed for harmony, security, and goodwill. We both vowed to try our best.

During that week, I was urged to let go with love and compassion. To accept that although I could support my husband's recovery, I couldn't fix him. Instead, I'd best concentrate on fixing myself. Terry and I would have to learn how to strip ourselves naked and swim in fresh water.

In a scene from the movie *When a Man Loves a Woman*, the alcoholic wife, Alice, fresh from the treatment center, decides to separate from her husband. In a rooftop scene with the San Francisco skyline as a backdrop, she explains that she can't remain in their roller-coaster relationship, where they break up and make up and break up again. Like Alice and her husband, Terry and I had become addicted to one another: high between binges and low immediately after. Our drama made us feel alive. Clearly it was veering out of control. Could treatment avert a tsunami?

During the final week, the counselors constructed an elaborate aftercare plan that included attending ninety twelve-step meetings during the first ninety days of recovery, finding a sponsor, and working the Twelve Steps of recovery. In his self-assessment, Terry resolved to "make sure that I'm not lying to myself and to create an atmosphere of trust."

Before I left, Terry gave me a sealed envelope. "Here, read this when you get home. Don't forget to walk Lucky. Say 'hi' to Matt. I miss him, too. See you in a week. You know that I love you." He smiled and whispered in my ear. "Honestly and truly, Frannie. Honestly and truly."

Minutes after leaving the treatment center, I pulled my car to the side of the road and read Terry's note:

Admitting to myself that I am powerless over alcohol was and is the most difficult thing I've ever done or experienced. I believe in self-awareness and responsibility. Finally confronting and admitting my alcoholism is psychologically devastating. I have never felt lower, more anxious, or less of a person. I do not have the personal power to control my drinking. Years of denial have only made my illness worse and wasted valuable time. Two years ago my wife tried to confront me with the problem. Instead of admitting alcoholism then, I compromised and pledged "to limit" my drinking. At first it seemed to work; however, on isolated occasions I drank to the point of passing out. And, eventually I "forgot" my pledge of self-control and began to drink more, more frequently. This affected my personality, particularly with my family, and my health. Managing my day-to-day life became increasingly harder. When I allowed myself to assess my behavior, all I felt was self-disgust. My family was walking on egg shells and it was my fault. Finally, I could not manage the guilt, anger, and the fear that my drinking was endangering the viability of my family and my life. With help from my wife, I chose life over death. I had nowhere else to go and could fool my wife and myself no longer.

I returned to our mountain home high on hope for recovery and determined to change my behavior. I didn't doubt Terry's commitment to recovery or my ability to let go with love. Nor did I realize that the end of treatment was the first of many obstacles that would surface like an angry tide in our future. Recovery for both the addict and loved ones requires constant work and vigilance, especially during that critical period after treatment.

PART III

Turbulent Water

THE ADDICT EXPERIENCES INCREASING TOLERANCE.

CRAVINGS SKYROCKET, THE BODY DETERIORATES,

THE DRUG DICTATES. THE ADDICT BECOMES ISOLATED

FROM FAMILY AND FRIENDS.

DARK WINE WATERS

CHAPTER SEVEN

Sinking

From saying to doing is a long stretch.

Italian proverb

In those first few weeks after treatment, I melted into the glow of early recovery, naively expecting smooth sailing from then on. It would be a long time before I learned that treatment and recovery are two different matters of concern. However, in those early days, goodwill flowed between us, even and steady like the water in the creek beside our home on a tranquil August day. We reestablished our familiar routines and reawakened romance. Terry and I held hands on long walks, accompanied by Terry's beloved dog, Lucky, and talked about our future.

Nevertheless, I continued to stick my fork in his plate. "Oh, by the way, I picked up a schedule for you of twelve-step meetings in Charleston. I'll go dig it out of my book bag. You know I'm surprised there are so many meetings. It seems like a lot of people are in recovery."

"Thanks, Frannie. Just as soon as I'm caught up at work, I plan to get started. I promise."

"But at the treatment center they recommended ninety meetings in the first ninety days. In fact, they were pretty adamant about it."

"I'll look over the schedule and get on it as soon as I can. I promise."

About a week later, Terry announced that he had started to attend a noon recovery meeting on weekdays.

"It's only a few blocks walk from my office. I can use the exercise." On Saturday afternoon, he left for another meeting in Dunbar, a little town fifteen minutes away. "Want anything from the grocery store? I can stop at Kroger's on my way home." He didn't say much about the meetings. Though starving for details, I tried not to press him. Nevertheless, I continued to nibble from his plate.

One Sunday afternoon as we were heading for a matinee at the Park Place Cinema, I said: "I'm truly proud of you. Almost three months into recovery. Have you found a sponsor so you can begin working the steps?"

"I've met some nice people at the meetings, but I haven't connected with anyone yet. There's plenty of in-and-out. People come and go all the time. But don't worry. I'm sure to find someone eventually."

"At the treatment center they said it's especially important to find a sponsor right away."

"No offense, but sometimes you're too hung up on what the experts say. They also told me to find someone I feel comfortable with. You know, like a friend. Frankly, I'm not comfortable sharing intimate details with a stranger. Besides, I worked the steps at the treatment center. But I promise to keep an eye out. Don't worry so much."

I had been cautioned to watch for signs of relapse, like slacking off on meetings, not finding a sponsor, or failing to work the steps. Then again, I reasoned that treatment had been successful, and Terry was attending recovery meetings, or so I thought at the time. Besides, I wasn't about to let go of our post-treatment honeymoon. I failed to recognize that treatment isn't recovery and that life after treatment presented a different set of challenges, some larger than when the disease was active. I plunged into books and articles about relapse: causes, pitfalls, and ways to prevent one. Armed with this knowledge, I was determined that Terry wouldn't be ambushed. Once again, I fell into a codependent trap. I refused to let go.

Relapse has no schedule. It can occur at any time, but is more likely to happen during the first year of an addict's recovery. Sometimes a person enters recovery and never, ever leaves. In other cases, a person relapses more than once before finally "getting the program." What I know now, that I did not know back then, is that the relapse starts before you pick up the drink or drug. It starts when the addict lets up on his or her program of recovery, which may happen weeks or months before the substance or behavior is resumed. Sadly, it can also happen when a person never actually gives recovery a chance, which was the case with Terry, despite his good intentions. He never did find a sponsor or attend all the meetings he let me think he did.

As a result, Terry catapulted back into his disease quickly.

Except for an occasional movie with close friends, we kept to ourselves. Three months after treatment, we decided to resurface at a Halloween costume party hosted by friends from the university. Their gatherings were always lively. I squeezed into a Girl Scout outfit purchased at a secondhand store, and Terry donned a faded poncho from his college days. Although I doubted he'd wear it, I borrowed a sombrero from a friend at work.

"There," I said as I placed the hat on his head. "Perfect. You look like Pancho Villa." When we arrived at the party, he carried the hat from the car and placed it on top of a giant papier-mâché pumpkin in the front hallway.

"Pancho Pumpkin."

We entered the crowded family room with a bundle of apprehension, a bowl of potato salad, and a half gallon of Diet Coke. As we made our way to the deck on that unseasonably warm night, Dracula, Elvis, Miss Piggy, and other revelers greeted us warmly.

"Oh my God, is that you in that get up?"

"How's it going?"

"What have you two been up to?"

"Haven't seen you for a long time."

"Hey, *hombre*, you look great."

No one mentioned Terry's treatment.

As I placed my potato salad on the picnic table stacked with chips, dips, cheese and crackers, pasta and bean and fruit salads, and homemade brownies, cookies, and baklava, I spotted a keg of beer beside a barbeque grill in one corner of the deck. A cooler of ice filled with soft drinks, more beer, and liters of wine sat beside it.

Terry and I circulated separately. Out of habit, or maybe fear, I kept one eye on him and the other on the keg and ice chest. Sipping Diet Coke, he huddled with the guys to dissect calls, fumbles, and scores of college and pro football games, including play-by-play moves of his beloved Dallas Cowboys. (An avid fan, he read *Sports Illustrated* from cover to cover each week.)

He appeared comfortable and, as best I could tell, hadn't approached the keg or ice chest. I relaxed, sipped white wine, and caught up with neighbors and friends. But since I was incubating a cold, I was tired and decided we should leave early, but that I would leave by myself if Terry didn't want to depart yet.

I pecked Terry on the cheek and whispered, "I'm feeling tired. Jay and Mindy are getting ready to leave, so I'll catch a ride with them. I might still be up when you get home. If not, I'll see you in the morning."

"Okay, I won't be too long."

I waited until midnight, and when he hadn't arrived, I went to bed. I stirred when Terry eased into bed beside me. The red numbers on the digital clock registered 1:15 a.m. I slept again, fitfully. Early the next morning, I woke up to find Terry flat on his back at the edge of the bed with one leg dangling onto the floor. I shook him. He roused slightly and mumbled, "What is it?" His eyes were bloodshot and he smelled of liquor. With my heart racing, I fled to the kitchen, grabbed a pack of cigarettes, reheated a pot of coffee, and headed to my study where I let loose in my journal, which doubled as a bitch-and-groan book.

Here's a sample:

> You're passed out and ask, 'What is it?' How could you do this again?

> I had to resist the urge to scream at you. Instead, I write. Better to scream on paper than in person. Right now I'd like to chisel open your skull and pour in a gallon of sanity because I can't handle this craziness again. The lies, the tension, the pleas, the tug of war between us.

Then I listed two pages of invectives, beginning each sentence with "I'm angry because:

> ...you won't open up...haven't found a sponsor...aren't working the steps...and have broken the promises you made before we left the treatment center."

I was angry because he'd relapsed so quickly, though later I discovered this wasn't uncommon. (I even learned of a young man who relapsed the exact day he left a treatment center after a six-month stay.) I was angry at myself for having believed that Terry was truly committed to recovery.

I ripped the pages from my journal, sealed them in an envelope and then propped it on the kitchen counter. I dumped an ashtray full of cigarette butts into the garbage and headed to my office, where I spent the afternoon grading papers, seething, and smoking.

When I returned home, Terry was gone. The envelope lay on the kitchen counter. On the back of it he'd written:

"I'm truly sorry that I messed up. I don't want to shut you out. I am trying. I'll do everything I can to stay sober from now on. I love you."

Sadly, he was unable to surrender. Even after a month in a residential treatment program, he still believed that he could do it himself. At that point, I didn't surrender either.

Although I nagged Terry about going to recovery meetings, I didn't join one of the twelve-step programs for family and friends of addicts. Looking back, I regret that I resisted recovery for so long. Had I been working a program, I could have avoided unnecessary heartache both for myself and my husband. What is that old cliché about knowing more and doing better?"

Three months after his treatment, Terry and I jumped back into a stormy sea. When you bodysurf into the rhythm of a smooth wave, the ride lasts for some seconds. Your blood pulses, senses heighten, memory sharpens, energy peaks, and pleasure chemicals flood your brain. But if the sea is rough, the wave's velocity sucks you under and batters your body. Fear floods your brain. Terry and I hurtled up and down between tranquil and turbulent. From exuberant sex to icy silence, from candlelight dinners to meals we could barely digest, from laughter to arguments, from goodwill to rancor, from hope to despair.

We created the illusion of recovery and, once again, settled into managing the disease, even though our lives had become unmanageable. We thrived on passion and pain. Our melodrama sustained us.

Terry continued to drink. I continued to enable and deny. After all, he didn't miss work, he paid our bills on time, helped with household chores, stayed in touch with Zinna, watched football games with Matt, and spent time with friends. Besides, his episodes were never sprees or benders. The "lamp shade on the head" performance wasn't his style. Whether drunk or sober, my husband was never raucous, rude, surly, or loud. Always a Southern gentleman. Never nasty. He simply dissolved, like early morning mist hovering over the river that runs through our town.

In the aftermath of one prolonged week of frigid silence, I approached him, my voice steady and smooth. "You know that we can't go on like this much longer. It's too painful. I don't understand. Why do you continue to drink when so much is at stake?"

"Oblivion, Frannie," he answered. "I like the oblivion."

DARK WINE WATERS

CHAPTER EIGHT

Smooth Water

Talk doesn't cook rice.

Chinese proverb

Burdened with the fallout from intermittent binges, we journeyed toward middle age. I campaigned for a family therapist.

"We need someone objective to help us sort our concerns out." Although no Freudian, I had faith in the talking cure. Terry was less sanguine. He often said, "Talk is overrated."

"That's funny coming from a lawyer."

"Exactly," he'd reply.

"Terry, I know you're trying, but you're still drinking and it's still interfering with our lives. It's painful and frustrating for both of us and for Matt too, even though he's away at college. We need help. I want you to consider our seeing a therapist for a few times. We need help. Will you think about it?"

"Look, I'll give the recovery meetings a try again."

"But you haven't gone in a long time."

"Yeah, I know. I need to go back."

I flirted with a twelve-step fellowship myself. At the few meetings I attended, I found myself pitying those poor souls who *really* had problems. I couldn't (or wouldn't) identify with their sad stories of abuse, suspended driver's licenses, broken marriages, lost jobs, bankruptcy, welfare or, worse yet, jail. Those events had nothing to do with Terry and me. We were as far removed from those catastrophes as the beach from the mountains. We were successful professionals with a four-bedroom house in the suburbs, two late-model cars, a kid in college, a plethora of friends and acquaintances, an annual vacation at Holden Beach, and even some money in the bank. Besides, nothing I heard or read in the pamphlets I picked up at those meetings had helped me get my husband to stop drinking. Instead, I heard countless platitudes about turning my will and life over to a Higher Power and a bunch of inane slogans. The program wasn't for me. I opted for therapy instead.

Now I understand that we didn't need therapy. Terry needed to stop drinking. I needed to let go. We could have benefited from a twelve-step program. But we weren't ready. I was unwilling to let go of control, and Terry was unwilling to let go of drinking. You can't force recovery. You have to be willing to surrender.

So, after yet another scene, I mentioned therapy again. "We need to get some help. I don't want to beg and plead with you. It's degrading. You don't have to commit to anything long term. I'm asking you to agree to come with me for a few sessions."

To placate me, Terry agreed to show the flag.

Committing to therapy is one thing, but finding the right therapist is another. A few colleagues in the psychology program at the university recommended several therapists. I contacted one whom I heard worked with alcoholics. He charged on a sliding scale and was available to meet with us. I felt confident, that after a few sessions, Terry would stop drinking. That simply.

Lenny's office was large, with a high ceiling, tall windows, and minimal furnishings: a worn vinyl sofa, two end-tables, and plastic trash container, built-in cabinets and bookshelves lining one wall. Like an astute librarian, I scanned book titles and considered it a good omen when I spotted several by Carl Jung. Perhaps we'd dissect our archetypes or delve into the collective unconscious. A few photos were scattered on the shelves. A glossy black and white of a young man sporting Groucho Marx glasses and a rubber nose with bright eyes shining under a mop of curly black hair made me smile.

During our sessions, Lenny sat in an Eames chair behind his large wooden desk. The chair was too small for his bulky frame. He shifted his weight frequently. From day one, Terry and I stationed ourselves on opposite ends of the sofa across the room from him. Perhaps it was the high ceilings or too much empty space, but I felt that Lenny sat too far away from us.

Despite the physical distance, the three of us managed to make a connection quickly. Consider this: we talked for fifty minutes a week, for approximately two and a half years. That's an enormous amount of mediated dialogue.

What I most recall is the tone and texture of those sessions. The chill in the room. The pale light of late afternoon. Lenny's corny jokes. His empathy. Terry's soft voice. My tears. Our fears. And hope.

A few sessions stand out. Once when Terry was out of town, Lenny and I discussed Terry's relationship with his mother.

"You know, Fran, like most men, Terry learned how to relate to women through his relationship with his mother," Lenny explained. I told him about Zinna's decision to divorce Rex when he wiped out the family savings and went on a weeklong binge with his brother. Terry was only two years old. We talked about how his mother devoted her life to her only child and sent unspoken messages. "Don't make waves," (because you will upset me). "Don't disappoint me," (because you're my life). "You're the man of the house, be good, be perfect." She sacrificed to support him and didn't complain. Like most parents, she did the best she could.

"Let me tell you a story," I said. "It's about Terry's senior prom. He didn't have a date but he didn't want to disappoint his mother. So he lied. He rented a tux and bought a corsage. Hanging in Zinna's living room is a large black and white photo of Terry promenading out the front door, smiling, wearing the tux and carrying the corsage box. Instead of the prom, he went to the movies, maybe saw a double feature. I'd bet he looked out of place sitting there wearing a tux. To this day Zinna believes that Terry and his 'date' slow danced at the Thomas Jefferson High School senior prom."

"When he told me that sad story, I asked him why he didn't simply tell his mom the truth. After all, not everyone goes to the prom. It's no big deal. He said his mother wouldn't have understood and that he didn't want to disappoint her. You know, Lenny, my parents would have understood, and even if they hadn't, I doubt that I'd have lied to them."

"Fran, let me put it this way: While your way and his mother's way are different, the result's the same. Her expectations were largely unspoken. You confront and challenge. Same outcome— he retreats. You're like a B-52 bomber and he's like a donkey. He could never meet his mother's expectations. No one could. So he lied to protect himself. Now he lies to you and lies to himself too." Lenny continued, "Think of childhood as a journey on a ship. If the seas are rough, then people abandon ship. They take a life preserver to survive. The life preserver's a kind of coping mechanism in childhood. Like a pacifier or security blanket. When some people reach dry land, they hang on to the life preserver even when it's no longer functional. Terry's been clinging to that preserver for many, many years."

"So what do I do about it?"

"Try to understand and give it time. He's coming to sessions, going to meetings, and trying to stay sober. Be patient."

Since our ship was sinking, I clung to Lenny. But he couldn't save us because we were drowning in denial. Terry wouldn't surrender and I wouldn't let go.

He'd lied to Zinna about the prom, later he lied to me about attending twelve-step meetings, as I learned when I stumbled upon one of Terry's more ingenious subterfuges.

One morning I sifted through unpacked boxes stacked under the pool table in the basement looking for an old textbook. When I pried open the lid of one box, torn ticket stubs spilled out. Thousands of them. *What in hell?* I thought. Each stub was stamped "Mountaineer Race Track," a dog track close to our home. Fascinated, I plopped down onto the damp cement floor to examine this hidden treasure. For the next two hours, I organized the tickets by date. Like a bank teller tendering crisp bills, I methodically arranged them into separate piles: two-dollar bets, five-dollar bets, twenty-dollar bets, win-place-show, exactas, trifectas, and other combinations. I calculated that he bet approximately two hundred dollars on each visit. The dates covered a five-year period. Hours and hours of track time.

As I sat on the garage floor surrounded by those ticket stubs, I laughed and I cried. How could I have been so blind? How could he have been so devious? Why hide a box of losing ticket stubs? Why not tear them up and litter the track's infield, like the other gamblers? That's what my father and his cronies did at Aqueduct racetrack back in Queens.

Instead of attending recovery meetings, Terry went to the dogs. Literally. A few times, he mentioned some guy from the program who asked for a ride to the dog track because he didn't have transportation to get to work. And sometimes this guy gave Terry a hot tip.

"A sure thing, Frannie."

But Terry's gambling buddy remained anonymous, as did Terry's sponsor. He was vague about both. "I got started with one guy, but it didn't work out because of our schedules. Haven't connected with anyone else yet, but I'm sure I will. I need to give it some time."

On Saturdays before noon, he'd announce he was leaving for a meeting.

"Going to my meeting, Frannie." Sometimes he said that he'd run a few errands, or that he'd met his buddies for a quick round of par-three golf or gone for coffee after a meeting. I took him at his word.

Years later at a writing conference, I met a fifty-something blonde who also was drafting a memoir about addiction. During lunch, we recounted our respective battles like combat veterans. She outlined her life with an abusive alcoholic whom she divorced after twenty-five years of marriage. I confessed Terry's struggle with booze.

"Codependency," she said. "Don't you hate that word?"

"Yeah, and dysfunctional, enabling, controlling, and self-pitying. Self-pity. That was a huge one for me. Still bites me every once in a while."

"Honey, I don't know what you have to complain about. You told me a minute ago that your husband wasn't mean and nasty. It wasn't anything like I went through."

So her pain was worse than mine.

"Well, I guess it's all relative," I muttered as I bent over to grab my backpack. "Almost one o'clock. Time to get going. I need to pick up a book before I head to my next workshop." She and I both had much to learn; about identifying instead of comparing, and about other matters as well.

I avoided her for the remainder of the week, like I had avoided facing the full knowledge of Terry's obvious lies.

Avoidance: We codependents excel at it.

I turned the blonde woman's words over and over again in my journal. Terry *wasn't* nasty, and he *did* function extremely well between binges. Sometimes *months* passed without an incident.

Minimizing. We codependents are experts at that, too.

Did I expect too much? Sometimes I felt that Lenny thought I did. Still no matter how well our lives went between episodes, each binge rattled me. I couldn't shut my mouth. I wouldn't let go. I didn't trust God. Who needed God anyway? I was sure that I could fix Terry, make him stop drinking, and save our marriage. My willfulness would triumph. I may not have liked the word codependent, but I certainly was one. I had it all; Avoidance, minimization, and willfulness. The codependent's trifecta. Today I hang onto the slogan "Progress not perfection" whenever my willfulness surfaces. Looking back, I recognize my pride and arrogance.

I recall one session when Lenny said, "You know, Fran. You could do with some humility." Taken by surprise, I shot back.

"What exactly do you mean? You want me to be humble like the saints? You want me to wear a hair shirt? Flagellate? Do penance? What have I done to deserve this?"

"No. I specifically want you to think about humility. We can talk about it during our next session."

Fat chance, I thought.

"Maybe there won't be another session." Like a seven-year-old spanked for her naughtiness, I sulked for the rest of the hour. Lenny ignored me and turned his attention to Terry. Probably told one of his corny jokes to dispel the tension.

As Terry and I climbed into our Taurus, I ranted: "Who the hell does he think he is? Humility! What did he mean by that? What kind of advice is that? Does he think I'm arrogant, smug, selfish? You know, Terry, I'm not sure I want to continue. I'm truly disgusted."

"Calm down, we can talk about this later. I'm late for work."

I raged for the rest of that day. Even consulted an unabridged dictionary, a birthday present from Terry many years before. Like a conscientious student, I copied entries on the origin, definition, and nuances of the word "humble" in my journal:

Humble: modest or meek in spirit, manner, or appearance; not proud or haughty, synonym: lowly, an absence of vanity and pride, feeling of weakness or lack of worth.

Humble, humility. How dare Lenny say that to me? Doesn't he know what I've been going through? Haven't I poured my heart out week after damn week? The same thing over and over. 'Be patient, Terry's trying,' he says. 'You have to give him credit for trying.' Well, what about me? Is anyone giving me any credit for hanging in all these years, for making excuses for him, for sacrificing, for hoping and praying for miracles? Alcoholism isn't about humility; it's about being humiliated. And it's exhausting, too. I'm tired of dysfunctional. The truth is that I'm tired of little or no progress, of moving one step forward and two steps back, or riding into one stormy crisis after another. I'm tired of making excuses for him, telling lies, walking on egg shells, fighting and making up, careening from despair and hope. I'm tired of living like this.

But Lenny had hit a bull's eye. That's why it hurt so much. Though I never denied Terry's disease, I'd perfected the art of damage control. My "good cop" trumped my husband's weakness and vulnerability. (*"Don't lie to me; I know you were drinking last night. Admit it. God damn, would you just admit it?"*) Dressed in my God suit, fired up by self-righteousness, and nourished by my inflated ego, I contributed to Terry's punishing shame and guilt. Most damaging, I came to distrust not only my husband but myself.

A few months after the "humility" session, we received a phone call informing us that Lenny had died of a heart attack while he was out of town at a conference. His body was discovered in a hotel room two days after he died. A few weeks later we attended a healing session with his other clients. Our grief was as painful as the hard metal chairs we arranged to form a circle. We shared stories, memories, jokes, and anecdotes. Someone read a poem. To dispel some of the tension at the end of the memorial, Terry told one of Lenny's corny jokes. No doubt Lenny and the angels had a good laugh.

Although the staff at the counseling center offered to match us with another therapist, Terry and I never returned. Why continue? Neither Lenny nor I could get Terry to stop drinking. And neither Terry nor I was ready to surrender.

DARK WINE WATERS

CHAPTER NINE

Treading Water

Take rest, a field that has rested gives a bountiful crop.

Ovid

In 1993 I decided to walk away temporarily from our crazy-making. That year marked a significant milestone: my twentieth anniversary of teaching. I was granted a sabbatical leave. I craved writing time and a respite from teaching and Terry.

A colleague, Rick, at the University of Pittsburgh invited me to spend a semester on campus as a visiting scholar, a dubious title, as far as I was concerned. Although I would be visiting, I certainly thought of myself as no scholar. However, armed with a faculty library card and a tiny office in Pitt's renowned Gothic Revival Cathedral of Learning, I felt sufficiently scholarly to tackle the business at hand: to write daily, catch up on professional reading, attend lectures and seminars, and hang out on campus.

Although emotionally exhausted, I wasn't ready to end my marriage. But could I remain if the drinking continued? Did I still love my husband? Was love enough? If we stayed together, could

I let go? Could I face the pain of another divorce? What about finances and facing my future alone? What about Matt? I knew that he loved Terry despite problems caused by the drinking. "Mom," he would say, "I don't understand why he doesn't stop." "Me, too," I'd answer.

And what if Terry entered and stayed in recovery? Since drinking had charted his journey since college, what would happen if my weary traveler embraced recovery? Would he become an insufferable twelve-step zealot? A colorless character? Or a better version of himself?

Planning my sabbatical in Pittsburgh challenged us both. However, from the first, Terry supported me. "You've wanted long stretches of time to write. There'll be some hassles putting this together, but we'll handle it. You need this. You deserve this. I'll help you all the way."

And he did.

The sabbatical was to begin in January. In late October, we headed north on I-79 to Pittsburgh, a city crisscrossed with bridges spanning the Allegheny, Monongahela, and Ohio Rivers. I needed to find a clean, furnished, affordable rental in a safe neighborhood with access to public transportation and a short-term lease—doorman optional. Of course, this domicile existed only in my imagination.

Upon arrival we hit the classifieds in the newspaper. While I sipped coffee from a Styrofoam cup and Terry downed a Diet Coke during breakfast at the modest inn, we circled potential rentals and phoned for appointments, confident that we'd be plunking down a security deposit that day.

"Let's go, Frannie, we're gonna find you the right place."

With a city map and copy of the *Pittsburgh Post-Gazette* in hand, Terry navigated as I maneuvered from one Pittsburgh neighborhood to another: from Shadyside to Squirrel Hill to

Oakland. At our first stop, the swarthy landlord ushered us into a dank basement flat with a "kitchenette" stuffed into one corner of the dark wood-paneled living room. This skid-row special rented for five hundred a month. We catapulted out of there before viewing the bedroom and bath. Terry patted my shoulder: "Don't be upset. It's only the first one on our list. We'll find something."

"My God, if that place rents for five hundred, I'll have to camp out in a homeless shelter."

"Yeah, or the stacks in the Pitt library."

"Very funny."

"Only kidding."

We raced from one address to another, getting lost several times. One reasonably decent place had already been rented, and the others were too expensive. Several hours later, empty-handed, we decided to head back home. While trying to find my way from Oakland to downtown, I drove down a one-way street in the wrong direction. The front end of the Protégé went nose-to-nose with a rusty Volvo, whose driver honked and gave me the finger. Shaken, I parked the car and turned the keys over to Terry, who hated city driving. Nonetheless, without a word, he took the wheel.

Inside the Fort Pitt Tunnel, Terry zigzagged through a maze of lanes while I called out directions.

"There's the sign for I-79, can you get over?

"I'll give it a try."

He jumped two lanes and we headed south.

And as we drove back home, Terry kept the faith. "Frannie, don't get discouraged. This was our first try. We'll go back next weekend. We'll call a rental agent and check back at the housing office at the university. Maybe Rick will come up with something. He said he'd be on the lookout."

"I don't know. Either the apartments are gross or the rent is too high."

"You know we could up your housing budget if we have to. Don't worry. I checked—most sabbatical expenses are tax deductible."

I must have looked skeptical.

"It's true. Rent, mileage, even food," He grinned.

"That's right," he said. "You professors get all the breaks. Come on, lighten up. I'm hungry. Let's stop at that Greek place. What's the name of that place? You remember?"

Remarkably, with only a vague memory of the name to guide us, we found the restaurant. After stuffing ourselves on moussaka and baklava, we headed home.

During the following week, I pondered my Pitt plan.

"Look, Terry, I don't think it's worth it. Finding a place is taking too much time and energy. Housing is too expensive. I should probably stay put."

He shook his head and brought me a cup of herbal tea.

"Don't worry; we'll find something."

A few days later I received a call from an acquaintance who was a textbook representative based in Pittsburgh. During our conversation I shared my housing predicament. She mentioned that a professor friend and her husband were leaving on sabbatical in January. "They haven't rented their house yet. It's in Oakland. In fact, it's in walking distance to the university. Only blocks away from the Cathedral of Learning. You might give them a call."

That evening I phoned and set up an appointment. The day after Thanksgiving, Terry and I again headed north. "I have a good feeling about this," he said, as we entered the I-79.

The brick three-story on Lytton Street was enormous, with high ceilings and cavernous rooms: a large entry foyer, two living rooms, a kitchen with a breakfast nook and a separate butler's pantry, dining room and half bath on the first floor; four bedrooms and a full bath on the second; and a recreation room, office, and large bathroom with a claw-foot tub on the third. The rooms were cluttered, the curtains tattered, the carpet stained, and the furnishings mismatched. Books spilled from myriad shelves, and family photos covered the walls. The place was charming in a funky, haphazard way. We loved it.

The forthright owner, Tina, took us on a quick tour, pointing out her daughters' puppet theatre, art work, and handicrafts. Although the girls were grown and on their own, their childhood artifacts filled the rooms. It seemed as if they'd bounce in through the back door at any moment, giggling and laughing.

After the tour, Tina served tea. We sat on a banquette in the breakfast nook, with the girls' mobiles, tangles of construction paper and faded yarn, hanging from the low ceiling overhead. A floor-to-ceiling cork bulletin board was covered with the girls' art work. We chatted. Finally, Tina addressed the business at hand. Rent. "It's eight hundred dollars, all utilities included. You'd have to take care of my cats, Josephine and Cleo."

Terry and I exchanged a telling glance, knowing full well that we couldn't afford it.

"That's certainly reasonable, given the size and location. Can we think about it and get back to you later this week?" I asked.

"Sure. But I want you to know that a young couple with a new baby is coming by tomorrow. They're from the university."

As we walked toward our car, Pitt's landmark Cathedral of Learning loomed ahead, towering above that urban campus. "Well, that's it. We can't afford it, and I don't need all that space. Besides, they're sure to rent the house to the couple from the university. Let's forget it. I'm going to stay in Charleston. I can write at home and do research in the library."

"Don't give up yet, Frannie. Maybe we can figure out how to swing the rent. You wouldn't have to pay for parking or transportation; the campus is in spitting distance."

"It's impossible. I'm staying home. I'll manage," I replied.

Later that week, Tina called. "Fran, we want you to have the house, and I think that I found a way for you to manage the rent. We have a friend whose son needs a temporary place to stay. If the truth be known, his mother feels he's too comfortable in his nest. We could rent him the third floor for $250 a month and you could pay the difference. You'd have to share the kitchen with him, but that shouldn't be a problem. I need your decision in the next two days."

I hung up and phoned Terry at work.

"Grab it," he said.

So on January 10, Terry and I headed back to Pittsburgh. As we exited the Fort Pitt Tunnel, the cityscape bloomed in front of us. It felt as if I could stretch out my hand and touch window panes of the Pittsburgh Glass Building.

"Wow, Ter, look at that. The city's right in your face."

Our tiny Protégé was packed with my cumbersome computer and printer, four heavy boxes of books and journals, suitcases packed with winter clothing, pillows, sheets and towels, and photos of Terry, Matt, and Lucky. As Terry carried the book boxes up two flights of stairs, he teased, "Don't they have books at the Pitt library? Why did you bring all this paraphernalia?"

"Because I plan to catch up on my reading."

I never opened those boxes. Terry lugged them back down two flights of stairs the following May. But I was far from idle. I camped out at the Hillman Library in carrel # 336 with its floor-to-ceiling window overlooking busy Forbes Avenue. Sometimes I wandered to the airy second floor that housed a special collection of books; most often I meandered through the open stacks. My reading choices were as haphazard as the décor of Tina's house and leaned toward what Terry called "those metaphysical miseries."

Authors like theologian Ted Peters, poet May Sarton, new-age guru Deepak Chopra, and Carl Jung filled the shelves in my carrel or were laid on my bedside table. One weekend I reread

Viktor Frankl's *Man's Search for Meaning*, which Terry had given me shortly after we began dating. On many forays to the Pitt bookstore, I discovered the Buddhist monk, Thich Nhat Hanh. I even dipped into a used copy of *The Tibetan Book of the Dead*.

At the Western Psychiatric Library on the far end of campus, I devoured volumes on alcoholism and filled my journal with copious notes, quotes, and reflections, as if I were conducting research for a dissertation.

I read about the etiology of alcoholism, which continues to elude researchers, about the "alcoholic treatment jungle" and the high rate of relapse. I learned that "systems theory" downplays alcoholism as a disease of the individual, and points the "sickness" finger at the family. I recognized myself as one of those "wives who fail to make good on their threats to leave and so help perpetuate the drinking." I shifted through jargon such as "cognitive dissonance," which is waging an internal battle when your philosophy of life conflicts with your reality; "scale-tipping incidents, last straws, or clinchers," like drunk driving; and "catch 22s," when the spouse fears that she's losing her mind because the drinking continues in spite of the alcoholic's continuing denials. In a nutshell, the researchers concluded that alcoholism is a "complex phenomenon with its combination of free will and compulsion, as well as its physiological and psychological aspects."

Yet, these volumes of facts, findings, and advice didn't assuage my confusion and indecisiveness: Do I stay married or seek a divorce? Searching for a definitive answer, I constructed elaborate pro and con lists and wrote in my journal. However, my categorical tug of war always ended in a deadlock. An excerpt:

Maybe I should try the codependents' twelve-step group again. But listening to those stories depressed me; all of those horrendous situations. I couldn't identify with those people. And all those slogans and platitudes. And they didn't provide any help on how I can get Terry to stop drinking.

All they kept saying is if you work on yourself things will change. Well, I don't have the problem. He does. He sure as hell provides many opportunities to get me worked up, like when he breaks his promises or tries to manipulate me with those damn allergy excuses. What a ruse. I'm not even sure if he goes to the meetings like he says. The truth is I can't trust him. I don't want to live in fear. Day in and out waiting for another shoe to fall. The perpetual storm at sea. Then again when he's sober, he's so considerate and caring. And even when he's drunk, he's never nasty or unkind. When he's drunk his moods shift, he broods and becomes unavailable. I should be able to handle his drinking because when it's good between us, it's very good. Right now I miss him very much, but I'm grateful to have this space to sort things out.

In retrospect, my journal reflections were nothing more than pretext. The confessions of a confused codependent who refused to let go. I was as addicted to Terry as he was addicted to alcohol. Even at that point in our marriage, I would not admit that I was powerless and needed help.

During my sabbatical I scheduled several appointments with a therapist who had credentials in addiction treatment. A friend at Pitt recommended him. At one session he said, "Alcoholics are incredible liars. Did you know that some of them will swear they aren't drinking even though a urine sample tests positive?" Well, I never did ask Terry to take urine tests, but telling lies and keeping secrets, oh, yes, he did that frequently. Is denial a disease or a symptom of the disease? Does depression cause alcoholism or does alcohol cause depression? (Many addicts have mental health problems that the experts tag as dual diagnosis or co-morbidity.) And what's the distinction between helping and enabling? And how does someone stand by and watch a loved one destroy himself?

Every three weeks Terry made the four-hour drive north from our mountain home. I looked forward to his weekend visits when we'd explore the city together. At the Carnegie Museum we wandered through a John Muir Yosemite Exhibit with photographs by Galen Rowell. We marveled at photos of majestic sequoias that had lived for three thousand years. "Wow," I said, squeezing Terry's hand. "That is hard to imagine." At the museum gift shop, he purchased a coffee table book of Galen photos for me. I still have it. Afterward we strolled to Paradise Café for biscotti and cappuccino.

Saturday afternoons we poked around Borders Bookstore. Terry even agreed to sit through a poetry reading at Hemingway's Bar. Some Sunday afternoons he'd watch the Dallas Cowboys game while I busied myself in the kitchen.

On "the Strip," an ethnic enclave near downtown, we shopped for imported olive oil, Genoa salami, fresh prosciutto, and creamy ricotta at the Macaroni Company, one of many traditional food stores in that part of town. The smell of pungent black olives and sharp cheeses took me back to my childhood in New York.

"Look at the fresh cannoli," I swooned. "We had cannoli for dessert at my grandmother's on special occasions. If only we had one decent bakery in Charleston," I lamented.

In my Pitt photo album, Terry and I stand in front of Paninni's Bakery, each hoisting a loaf of crusty Italian bread like Oscar winners displaying their trophies. One frigid Saturday afternoon we warmed up on minestrone and savored thick slices of Italian bread while a continuous melody of Frank Sinatra classics played at The Italian Oven restaurant.

In Oakland, we strolled down Forbes Avenue and sampled French fries at The Original Hot Dog Shop, a Pitt landmark. We toured the Cathedral of Learning with its dark, Gothic first floor and peeked into the Nationality Rooms. I couldn't figure out how students read their textbooks in that dim light. Since Terry was a sports nut, we checked out the old Forbes Field and located a plaque that "marks the spot where Bill Mazeroski hit a homerun ball that cleared the left center field wall of Forbes Field on October 13, 1960, thereby winning the World Series championship for the Pittsburgh Pirates." I treasure a photo taken at that historic 457 foot wall; Terry bends from the waist, as he leans forward pretending to catch a fly ball in the outfield. His eyes sparkle as he laughs into the camera. This was the playful Terry whom I loved. Why did his disease change him into a humorless, empty shell?

Film buff Terry was delighted to learn that Gene Kelly was a Pitt alumnus—*Singing in the Rain* was one of Terry's favorite movies. We enjoyed other movies, too, during that time: One Saturday afternoon at a downtown theatre we laughed to tears during *Johnny Stecchino* (Johnny Toothpick) about a bus driver who doubles as a Sicilian mobster.

"You crazy Italians," Terry shook his head. "More colorful than the Southern Baptists."

"I don't know about that . . ." I kidded back.

One evening we rode the tram to the top of Mt. Washington, a section that overlooks the city, and ate dinner at the Georgetown Inn. We lucked into a front row table and gazed down at the Ohio River and the bridges that spanned it. Bathed in candlelight, we sparkled like the lights shimmering over the water below.

Although we had to stretch our budget to celebrate our fourteenth wedding anniversary on March 30, Terry made reservations at the Grand Concourse, an upscale restaurant at Station Square. We always celebrated two anniversaries, March 30, our wedding day and October 3, the day we met, when Terry had brought me chestnuts.

Sometimes we hung out at the house, sipping hot chocolate in front of a blazing fire and paging through the family's many photo albums. Usually, sweet Josephine jumped on our laps and purred. Her sister, Cleo, ventured out only during feeding time.

Otherwise, she remained undercover, including the time she hid in the rafters in the garage.

On Sunday mornings, we made love and lazed in bed. Before heading home, Terry often fixed ham and cheese omelets, served them with fresh muffins and pastries from the grocery store. Then he'd stuff the sports pages in his small duffel, kiss me good-bye, and head out the front door. When he drove away in his dirty Taurus, I'd feel empty. How could I ever imagine divorcing this terrific guy?

Between Terry's visits I worked on my writing. But writing is lonely. Since I needed deadlines, guidance, and feedback, I signed up for two classes in nonfiction. On the first evening of a class in magazine writing, I panicked when I encountered a dozen eighteen-year-olds chatting and waiting for the instructor. I thought, *What am I doing with these kids? They must think I'm ancient.* I sat silent for the next two hours. When I returned home, I phoned Terry before even shedding my coat.

"I can't do this. The students are so much younger than I am and they seem to be smarter."

"Come on, are you going to let a bunch of kids intimidate you?"

He had a point.

So I hung in and drafted several articles. One was published in a slick magazine. Only a sidebar, but I received a check for $125. First time anyone paid me for my prose. No small thing for an insecure writer.

I felt more comfortable at a women's poetry workshop led by a gifted teacher at Carlow College. Each week some ten to fifteen middle-aged women squeezed around a conference table to share and critique drafts. I listened, learned, and drafted a few lousy poems.

Like a ravenous guest at a cocktail party, I sampled an assortment of lectures, readings, performances, and exhibits. At Pitt's visiting writer's program, I sat at the feet of Michael Pollan and Geoffrey Wolff. During "Sex Awareness Week" at Carnegie Mellon, the notorious Dr. Ruth held forth on masturbation and sexually transmitted diseases. I attended a chamber music concert by the Quartetto Gelato. At the Public Theatre I enjoyed a zany performance of *Evelyn and the Polka King*. Unfortunately, although I was in the neighborhood, I did not get to hear Fred (Mr.) Rogers give the commencement address at Pitt's graduation.

A few weeks before I was to head home, Cindy, one of my students who lived in Weirton, a town about twenty minutes from Pittsburgh, called to tell me that she was chaperoning the senior prom at the Sheraton Hotel in Station Square, and invited Terry and me to join her.

And so the night before my departure, Terry attended a senior prom, something he had missed when he was graduating from high school. We slow-danced under strobe lights in a dark ballroom packed with seventeen-year-olds resplendent in their formal attire, the sophisticated girls in their backless gowns, the awkward boys in ill-fitted tuxedos. Terry didn't wear a tux, and I didn't wear a gown or tiara. Nevertheless, when he surprised me with a corsage of pink roses, I felt like the prom queen. My king enjoyed himself as much as the departing seniors. Their lives loomed ahead, a blank canvas of possibility. Ours were more than half-over. Although our life was troubled, I didn't doubt our love. My five-month sojourn had provided the opportunity for a fresh start. So on Mother's Day of 1993, I returned to my mountain home and recommitted to my marriage vows convinced that recovery was still possible for Terry and me.

CHAPTER TEN

Storm Surges

If you understand, things are just as they are;
If you do not understand, things are just as they are.

Zen proverb

Like waves rushing to shore, we tossed and tumbled for the next three years: calm followed by storm followed by calm. After a binge, when Terry was slumped down in his Lazy Boy chair, I'd rant. "How could you? You told me you weren't drinking. You said you were going to meetings. You assured me you hadn't touched a drop while I was in Pittsburgh. Remember our last night there? How we walked along the river and talked about making a fresh start? No more drinking for you, no more nagging for me."

He sat still in his chair and said nothing. Why interrupt my dramatic monologues?

"Maybe I should have stayed in Pittsburgh. Maybe I should move there permanently. What would you care anyway? With me away, you could drink to your heart's content. Cat's away, mouse will play. You could drink up a storm; you could drink morning, noon, and night. I'm fed up, Terry, I'm absolutely fed up."

I swept out of the room like a diva making her dramatic exit. When I returned to the living room, he was gone. Who could blame him after that performance?

After a few days of frosty silence, we'd thaw and recalibrate our thermostats to a comfortable temperature. We'd leap from connect to disconnect, sometimes within hours. The drinking continued and the emotional fallout accelerated. After every episode, I either sank into bitter silence or simmered with rage. Hypervigilance became my watchword. My radar scanned for subtle shifts in his mood and behavior.

"Terry, something's off. You're not right. I can feel it."

"My eyes are red, but it's not what you think. The ragweed is killing me. You know how it is this time of year. I had to take an allergy pill."

"Look, we agreed that if you took a pill, you'd tell me so that we wouldn't get into it. I hate when you do this. And what's more, I hate these conversations. Over and over, the same damn conversation. When will it end? It's simple enough: Tell me when you take a pill, so that I know what's going on. I've asked you a hundred times. How many more times do I have to plead with you to simply tell me?"

"Sorry, I promise to fess up next time."

Often he couldn't "fess up" because he couldn't remember anything after a blackout. After work one evening, he carried home two jackets from the dry cleaner. While we cleared the dinner table, I asked, "Where did you put the clothes you picked up today?" He didn't respond. "I saw you carry the bag into the house. So where did you put it? For God's sake, Terry, can't you remember?"

At first, the blackouts were occasional, but as time passed, they increased in frequency. It took me a long time to recognize them for what they were. A blackout is a period of temporary amnesia. In the midst of one, an alcoholic functions as if he's aware of what's going on around him. Actually, he remembers nothing. So how does a partner cope with that?

Our seascape was either rough or calm depending on whether or not Terry was drunk. Life was marked by shutdowns, withdrawals, and tearful reconciliations.

Between storms, we functioned as well as, or maybe even better than our average, ordinary, normal, non-dysfunctional counterparts. This back-and-forth confused and frustrated me. During those times when Terry wasn't drunk, we embraced simple pleasures: steamy hot showers and back rubs, Saturday afternoon movies, poker and bridge with friends, and take-out pizza on Fridays after a busy work week. I remember how we savored the mellow sounds of Stan Getz as we sat shoulder to shoulder in front of a blazing fire or challenged one another in hotly contested games of Backgammon (Terry usually won). We mastered the basics of massage for couples but flunked ballroom dancing.

"Let's face it, Frannie; we're no Ginger Rogers and Fred Astaire."

In addition to our annual journey to Holden Beach, we bookended a few vacation days around our professional conferences. During a National Council of Teachers of English Conference in Baltimore, we stood in the square at the Inner Harbor and listened to a military band belt out *Give Me that Rock and Roll Music*. At the National Aquarium, I grabbed Terry's hand as we spiraled down a catwalk while sharks circled ceaselessly in dim light.

"You hungry?" Terry asked when we emerged from the darkness.

"Let's head over to Little Italy. It's only a few blocks away."

Like every area in every city that bears the name, Baltimore's Little Italy is replete with restaurants, often two or three on one narrow street. We strolled through the neighborhood and perused the menu outside Sabatino's. A white stretch limo was parked outside.

"Let's try it," Terry said. "If it's good enough for the mobsters, it's good enough for us." The minestrone and lasagna were as perfect as my Grandmother Francesca's. We topped off the evening with two scoops of gelato on sugar cones at Vaccaro's. I purchased two pounds of Italian macaroons—the kind I remembered, with the red and green cherries, and assorted biscotti carefully packed in a square paper box tied with string.

During a trip to Montana, we floated on an excursion boat on Flathead Lake. At Glacier National Park we walked through fern-covered trails, heavy with moss. The air sparkled and water rushed through streams and over falls everywhere. I felt right at home. Sitting on the top of a fire-engine-red double-decker bus, we traveled along the Going-to-the-Sun Road that cuts through the park to the visitor center at Logan Pass, snow covered in mid-May. I remember several tourists maneuvering through snow in sandals, while kids threw snowballs. Terry shot a picture of a mountain sheep climbing a steep rock face from the window of the bus.

On the second day of our stay at the YMCA Camp in Estes Park, Colorado, we adjusted to the thin air by drinking numerous glasses of water.

"Now, we know what John Denver meant by Rocky Mountain High," Terry remarked. We spotted our first moose grazing in front of the main lodge. "Boy, can you imagine one of those slamming into someone's car like the deer back home?" he said. "Some roadkill."

Maybe it was the altitude but I felt high on love for Terry during those days of magic in the magnificent Rockies.

In Seattle, at the Pike Street Market, we marveled at fresh fish packed in vats of shaved ice, and savored fresh king salmon baked on cedar planks around an open fire at the Tillicum Village Longhouse in Blake Island Park. At the cavernous Elliott Street Bookstore in the old section of town, we spent hours browsing shelves and stacks of books. From Seattle we hopped on a hovercraft to Victoria, British Columbia, with its ubiquitous totems and splendid harbor. There was water everywhere. I was enthralled. Although dressing up wasn't high on my husband's list, he donned a sports jacket and tie for high tea at the Empress Hotel, a landmark overlooking the harbor. At the Butchart Gardens, we stood in acres of waist-high tulips, a riot of pastel and primary colors stretching toward the sun in a cloudless sky. I swam laps at the large indoor pool in our hotel.

We also visited family during those years. My sister and brother-in-law and their five kids now lived in the bungalow where I'd grown up in Bayside, Queens. On our first visit, Terry was overwhelmed when everyone talked loudly at the same time. During Sunday dinner we squeezed around the dining room table and remained there for the next three hours.

"Terry, don't be shy. Eat. Eat. There's plenty. You want some more pasta? What about some meatballs? Fran loves my meatballs, don't you sweetie? I made them from Momma's recipe. How about some more sausage and peppers?" my sister asked as she sprang from kitchen to dining room, like a marionette, balancing bowls and platters. After the main course, she appeared with a large tray covered with cookies and pastries from Joe's Sicilian Bakery.

"Fran, I got the kind you like. Look, cassata cake exactly like grandma used to make. So, Terry, would you like espresso or do you want regular coffee? We got both."

"Carole, he doesn't drink coffee," I said.

She looked puzzled. "So what does he drink?"

"Sweetened ice tea." She shot me another look.

"We have lemonade. I think there's some ginger ale, too. But I can make some tea and put some sugar in it. How much?"

"Tons," I answered.

Terry experienced his maiden voyage on the subway into Manhattan.

"What a deal. I can't believe that millions of people ride these electric boxes to and from work every weekday!"

"This isn't anything. You can't imagine rush hour." During one visit, we treated my nieces, Patricia and Maria, then ten and eleven years old, to a weekend in the city: sightseeing at the Empire State Building, Museum of Natural History, FAO Schwarz, and riding a horse-drawn carriage through Central Park. As soon as I'd emerge from the subway into the street teeming with pedestrians, my body reflexively snapped back into Manhattan super-speed, which would give Terry a chuckle.

"Well, I guess you can take the girl out of New York, but . . . ."

At the end of each visit up north, I loaded up on Italian bread, gallon tins of olive oil, several dozen fresh bagels, and boxes of Joe's cookies and pastries. (Even today my sister is not allowed to cross the threshold of my home without these supplies.)

"Frannie, how are we going to carry all of this stuff on the plane? It may come as a surprise, but they sell food in West Virginia."

"Not food like this."

Terry felt comfortable with my boisterous family and was delighted when my nieces and nephews called him "Uncle Terry." But he didn't like the crowds, noise, and traffic in Manhattan, the island in a city that I adore. And while I felt welcomed by Terry's family in Texas, I didn't much like Dallas. In fact, I didn't like it at all.

"It's too big. There's a humongous church on every corner. Not to mention men with string ties and cowboy hats and boots, and women with enormous hair. And the politics. Don't get me started." As soon as my feet hit the ground at the Dallas/Fort

Worth Airport, I felt like one of those Fisher Price play-people placed in the center of a football field.

Even though Terry was nervous before every trip to Texas, our visits with his mom and aunt were pleasant.

In Dallas, we enjoyed a cuisine extremely different from the Italian meals we ate in Bayside. We always treated Zinna and Terry's beloved Aunt Frieda to dinner at El Fenix, a festive Tex-Mex eatery—in fact, a Texas tradition—with waitresses dressed in billowing skirts and colorful peasant blouses and Mariachi musicians wearing sombreros, who serenaded customers. We dipped supersized tortilla chips into spicy salsa and washed them down with sweetened ice tea. (Although I preferred a Dos Equis, I followed suit and ordered ice tea—unsweetened, with lemon and not too much ice.)

Terry's favorite cousin, Dinah, served up his favorites: super moist chocolate cake from Luby's Cafeteria and slabs of beef brisket slathered with sauce from Dickey's. "Not like that stringy stuff you get in North Carolina," Terry said as he placed a slice of brisket on white bread. At Highland Park Pharmacy on the corner of Knox and Travis Streets, we sat at the counter on chrome stools covered with red vinyl, ate grilled pimento cheese sandwiches on white bread, and sipped thick milkshakes from paper straws. The pharmacy was a second home to Terry, who had spent happy hours there after school reading comics and drinking cokes under the watchful eye of his beloved Uncle Donald, Aunt Frieda's husband. Donald had worked his way up from clerk to become a part owner of this neighborhood landmark. In deference to her Yankee daughter-in-law, Zinna served bagels and cream cheese for breakfast. And she always baked an apple pie. "Great pie, Mom, definitely the way I like it."

For his mother's seventieth birthday on July 26, 1994, we planned a special trip. "Pick a place you'd like to go, Mom, and

I'll take care of all the details." Zinna chose San Antonio, a fun city, but one to avoid when the thermometer registers ninety-nine degrees and you're pushing a wheelchair along the Riverwalk. Zinna had been diagnosed with MS at the age of fifty. Although she felt self-conscious in a wheelchair, she agreed to rent one to avoid fatigue while we were sightseeing. Although her left leg was weak and often painful, she never complained. To this day, I admire my mother-in-law's courage in the face of a debilitating condition.

At the Hertz car rental, Terry upgraded a compact to a Lincoln Town Car and struggled to park it near our first tourist attraction in downtown.

"Is that puny building the Alamo?" I gasped.

"No offense, but you are treading on mighty thin ground here. Don't forget that when the Republic of Texas became a state, its charter said that it could divide into five states. Still can."

"Is that a fact?"

"Hot damn, girl. I wouldn't lie about something as important as that," he winked.

After a short tour of that historic icon, we cooled off at an IMAX Theatre that featured a recreation of the battle of the Alamo. This epic played out on a six-story screen with six-track stereo sound: booming cannons, galloping horses, and the hordes of Mexicans storming the fortress. Terry leaned toward me and whispered, "Pretty impressive, don't you think?" I smiled and rolled my eyes.

But all wasn't pleasure trips, sightseeing, family visits, and fine dining during those final years. An undercurrent of avoidance and denial dragged us down.

The drinking escalated.

Blackouts increased.

We disconnected and reconnected, and endured. More struggling through storms than clear sailing.

A typical sequence involved tears, anger, and silence, followed by regret, guilt, shame, sorrow, forgiveness, and promises to try harder next time.

During the summer following my 1993 sabbatical, my left eye started to twitch. More exactly, the fold between my lower eyelid and cheek bone popped in millisecond bursts. Not unremitting like a toothache, but rather like a pulse that spiked under my eye on an erratic schedule. For the most part, I ignored it.

However, I couldn't dismiss the panic attacks that began at the start of that fall semester. On the evening of the first class, I chatted in the hallway with a colleague. Suddenly, my heart began to race. My breath failed. My heartbeat pounded "ratta-tat-tat," as if a jackhammer rammed the walls of my chest. Then, as quickly as the commotion started, it stopped.

"You all right? Can you handle class?" my friend Molly asked.

"I think so. Maybe it was something I ate. I need some water and air."

"You sure you're okay? You look awfully pale to me."

"I'm fine. I'm sure it's nothing. Maybe it's first-class-of-the-semester jitters," I smiled.

"Hardly. You're an old pro at this. Well, if you need anything, don't hesitate to interrupt me."

"Thanks."

I entered the classroom, wrote my name and the number and title of the course on the chalkboard, introduced myself, and handed out the syllabus.

"Everyone in the right place? Good. Let's begin."

Eye twitching, chest pounding, I managed to conduct that first class, and then a whole semester's worth of classes.

And while my eye continued to twitch and my chest to pound, Terry faced his own health crisis. In 1994, he was diagnosed with age-related macular degeneration (AMD), an untreatable disease that gradually destroys the macula, the central area of the retina, and slowly erodes central vision. Vision becomes distorted, like the blurred-out faces of real criminals on TV shows. It's common in the elderly, striking almost 40 percent of those seventy-five years or older. Terry was only forty-five years old when diagnosed. A few days after his initial appointment with an eye specialist, he shared the news.

"Do you want to talk about it?" I asked.

"There's nothing much to talk about. The doctor gave me some pamphlets, a chart to check my vision, and information about diet and vitamins. That's the thing and there's no cure."

"Well, the doctors should be able to do something."

"Best I can tell, they can't do much except monitor it. Doctor McElroy wants to see me every few months."

"Don't worry. We'll figure something out."

How could such a thing happen to someone who savored books, movies, and television? To someone whose career rested on reading legal statutes and writing briefs?

The doctor gave Terry an Amsler Grid, a checkerboard chart with a white dot in the middle to check for wavy or missing lines. Terry taped it to the inside door of the linen closet. Each morning he closed one eye and looked at the grid to monitor his eyesight. His doctor suggested loading up on antioxidants found in dark green fruits and veggies because some research showed it slowed AMD's progression. I searched vegetarian cookbooks for recipes to prepare kale, collard greens, and spinach, so they wouldn't taste too bitter or tangy, like most greens of the mustard family. I also filled the pantry with generous supplies of oranges, mangoes, sweet potatoes, and a plethora of vitamins. Although he was at heart a chicken-fried steak and potato man, Terry complied with this diet for the most part.

"I'm trying to keep the faith, Frannie, trying to keep the faith."

"Don't worry. Everything's going to be fine. We'll beat this."

While our health and megavitamin routine may have assuaged our fear that Terry would become blind, it couldn't mitigate the physical meltdown or emotional fallout from his years of alcohol abuse.

So there we were. Well into the downside of addiction's slippery slope and slammed by another incurable, progressive disease.

Increasingly depressed, Terry brooded and said little. It was as if a spark had gone out in him.

While his spark dimmed, mine ignited. Although I should have known better I couldn't keep my mouth shut. After a drinking episode, we'd dodge one another and trade cryptic remarks for a few days. Then, I'd think, *This is ridiculous!* and I'd approach him.

"We need to talk." How he must have dreaded those words.

"You know, I think that sometimes talk is overrated."

"That's kind of funny, coming from a lawyer. But it doesn't matter. We're pouting like children. Let's talk this out."

We'd usually settle at the kitchen table, Terry with his plastic mug filled with ice and Dr. Pepper and I with warmed-over coffee, the space between us stiff and heavy, as if encased in fog. Over the years, we'd become virtuosos, like actors performing the same scene night after night in a long-running play.

"I know you were drinking last night, so don't deny it."

"I swear to you, I wasn't. But I had to take a pill because my allergies were kicking up again."

Depending on the circumstance or my mood, this dialogue could drag on for several hours, often late into the night. My accusations: "I'm sick of having the same conversation about your allergy pills. You use them as a cover for your drinking." His denials: "I'm telling you the truth. I wasn't drinking. I took a pill because my nose was stuffed and I couldn't breathe."

I've since learned that Terry's self-delusion was pathological. He came to believe his own lies.

And I lied to myself as well because I thought I could fix him.

The line between reality and denial was distorted. Tragically, like Terry's eyesight.

We visited Dallas over the Thanksgiving holiday in 1996. On Friday evening, we headed for El Fenix with Zinna, Aunt Frieda, her daughter Dinah, and Helen, a family friend. The place was packed; the atmosphere festive. After placing his order of green enchiladas and sweetened ice tea, Terry whispered, "I have to go to the bathroom. Tell the waitress to put all the orders on one check. I'm paying. I'll be right back."

Ten minutes passed. He didn't return. My stomach chilled and my eye began to twitch. As we munched on chips and salsa, I half-listened to talk of Dallas traffic, family gossip, and Christmas plans. *Where in hell was Terry?* The waitress served our entrees, placing a platter of enchiladas, beans, and rice in front of an empty chair. Still no Terry.

"Go ahead and eat. Don't let your food get cold. I'm sure Terry will be back soon." I picked at my taco salad and scanned the crowded room. *No sign of him. What do I do?*

"Excuse me," I said as I pushed my chair away from the table. "I'll be right back."

I skirted the crowd and made it to the restaurant's entryway, looked around, walked outside. Back inside, I approached the maître d'.

"Look, my husband seems to have misplaced himself. He's short, about 5' 9", gray hair, bald on top. He wears wire-rim glasses and has on a gray windbreaker. If you see him, please come and get me. I'm in the back at a table near the archway. Thanks."

By the time I returned to the table, everyone had finished dinner.

"Delicious, delicious. But way too much food," his mom said. No one mentioned that the elephant had left the room and failed to return. Finally, I spotted him under an archway, blank eyes scanning for something to hold, like a lonely sailor on a long journey. I bolted from my chair and skipped around tables to reach him. Then I grabbed his arm, shifted his weight to my right shoulder and led him back to our table. He eased down into a chair, smiled and drank some ice tea. "Do you want me to ask the waitress to warm your food?" I asked.

"No, not hungry. My stomach. It's acting up."

Although I didn't recognize it at the time, he was in the midst of another blackout.

"Well, then, is everyone ready to go?" I asked. After paying the bill, I dug into Terry's coat pocket for the car keys. His cousin pushed Zinna's rented wheelchair to the handicapped ramp. Terry stumbled as he tried to guide his mother into the passenger seat. "Here, dear, hold my purse." She grabbed the corner of the open door and lifted her left leg into the space below the glove compartment. We drove home in silence.

I helped his mom make her way from the carport to the back door. Terry followed and grabbed a diet Coke from the fridge. "My allergies are furiously kicking up. I'd better take a pill and go to bed. See you gals in the morning." I said nothing. Zinna brewed a pot of herbal tea. At ten o'clock we watched Tom Brokaw deliver NBC's news. Then we hugged and went to bed.

The next morning, Terry emerged from a hot shower, peachy fresh and ready-to-go. "Who wants breakfast? I'll fix bacon and eggs, or treat you girls at the Pancake House. What'll it be? Mom, I need to stop by Lowe's to pick up that lamp and get that bulb to fix the light in the garage. You said you needed some mulch, too. I want to take care of everything before we leave."

Two weeks later, Terry celebrated his forty-seventh birthday, on December 7. "Pearl Harbor Day, Frannie. You can't ever forget it." Despite problems with his vision, his spirits were good. In fact, he wrote me a grace note on a sheet of loose-leaf to mark the occasion. Under the date, he wrote: *"This is my birthday gift to Fran."* The list, still tucked under the top drawer of my wooden jewelry box, reads:

I'm blessed by:

1. *More so than ever, getting control over my body chemistry,*

2. *Mom's seeming stability,*

3. *The love of my wife—for putting up with my ups and downs—realizing that the downs have been particularly upsetting to her for good reason, but no excuses for her disappointments in me (this may be the most important on my list),*

4. *I appreciate the steadfastness of old and new friends,*

5. *My stepson, Matt, getting along in the world in his own way—which is as it should be,*

6. *Our new house—even complete with its troubles,*

7. *Even with the hassles that Fran may not project, looking forward to adding a dog to our family,*

8. *Our health and commitment to going forward. I'm feeling blessed and not depressed.*

My eternal love to Fran,
T.

CHAPTER ELEVEN

At the Bridge

*Reflect upon your present blessings—of which
every man has many—not on your past misfortunes,
of which all men have some.*

Charles Dickens

Watching *It's a Wonderful Life* was one of our many holiday rituals, as was Matt and Terry's hunt for the perfect tree, and Terry's sumptuous brunch, prepared on Christmas morning. "So when do you want to watch the movie?" he'd ask as we wrapped presents to send to his family in Dallas. Every year, he scurried to UPS to ensure the gifts arrived on time. Sometimes, the postage cost more than the gifts.

"Finding time to watch the movie shouldn't be a problem; it's on twenty-four hours every single day in December," I answered.

"That's because the copyright lapsed in 1975. It's public domain. That means TV stations can show it free anytime they want to."

"You would think everyone in America has seen at it least twice by now."

"Don't be such a cynic, Frannie."

Ironically, the movie's climax involves a near-fatal suicide attempt. Despondent over a financial setback at his family's bank, George Bailey (played by a young Jimmy Stewart) gets drunk at Martini's bar, survives a car crash, and staggers to the town bridge where he contemplates plunging into the icy river. His guardian angel, Clarence, rescues him. But an ungrateful George complains that it would have been better if he'd never been born at all. This inspires Clarence, who arranges to let George see what it would have been like if he had never existed.

After an otherworldly journey, George comes to recognize the difference he made in the lives of others. Transformed by this grace, he returns to his loving wife, Mary, and their four children. In the final scene, friends and neighbors gather and pool their money to save Bedford Falls from the evil Mr. Potter (a cantankerous Lionel Barrymore). George becomes the town hero, Clarence ascends to heaven where God rewards him with a set of wings, and the gang sings *Auld Lang Syne* in the closing scene. Terry informed me that the movie originally ended with Beethoven's *Ode to Joy*.

"You're kidding, right?"

"Scouts honor," he replied with a grin.

Like George Bailey, Terry wanted to be a hero. Once he confessed to me, "I want to be a hero in my own life." He loved movies and movie actors, particularly the Hollywood tough guys like Bogart, Cagney, and Garfield. Comparing himself to them, he came up short.

A child of Texas in the 1950s, he was weaned on TV Westerns, with hard-drinking, macho cowboys, like characters played by John Wayne. In fact, Terry's film archives contained collections of the Duke's B Westerns from the 1930s, such unmemorable films like *Blue Steel*, *Winds of the Wasteland*, and *Randy Rides Alone* (not to be confused with *Destry Rides Again*). *The Alamo*, that quintessential homage to Texas independence, is included. Wayne stars as Davy Crockett. I finally disposed of Terry's Davy Crockett coonskin cap, a childhood treasure, when it succumbed to mold. But his Davy Crockett scrapbook with faded photos of actor Fess Parker cut from the newspaper and pasted on black construction paper is buried in a trunk in the garage. No doubt in his fantasies, Terry morphed into a fast-draw gunslinger who upholds the law. He rides alone into town, strides into the saloon, downs a shot glass of whiskey, and single-handedly trounces outlaws with his fists. At the end of a brawl, he brushes off his britches, retrieves his hat, and climbs back on his horse (without falling on his face), and he rides into the sunset. A lawman who fights for justice and good. A tough guy who can hold his liquor.

Unlike his movie heroes, Terry couldn't "hold" his liquor and he couldn't control his drinking. Neither could his father. Like many adult children of alcoholics, Terry became a victim, too.

Christmas Eve was a watershed for George Bailey's family in the movie, as it was for us in 1996. We hosted our annual Christmas Eve open house. That year was special, our first holiday season in our new home. Matt, who was working in Geneva, Switzerland, flew home. That was to be the year we'd gather around the hearth to create glorious holiday memories.

After turning in my final grades for fall semester, I grabbed a wilted poinsettia and box of chocolates, gifts from students, and left for my three-week holiday break. Early the next morning, I began my yearly assault to prepare for the festivities. I vacuumed, mopped, swept dust balls from behind the refrigerator, dusted, waxed and rearranged furniture, and polished mirrors, brass lamps, and light fixtures. (Terry always swore that I'd emerged from the womb with a dust rag in my hand.) On subsequent days I baked and froze dozens of cookies, addressed a bundle of

Christmas cards, and purchased last-minute gifts, including a few generic ones, so I wouldn't be caught short.

The day before our open house, I polished silverware, hand-washed crystal goblets handed down from my mother, and white Lenox china from my grandmother. I ironed and folded holiday tablecloths and napkins, ordered a veggie tray from the supermarket and a centerpiece from the florist, positioned evergreen-and-bayberry-scented candles around the house, decorated the hearth with holly and hung our stockings with care. Both unwilling and unable to match my breakneck pace, Terry watched from the sidelines.

"I know enough to keep out of your way during one of your frenzies. Let me know when you need help."

On the morning of Christmas Eve, he rallied around 11:00 a.m. After allowing for the requisite half-hour he needed to wake and join the living, I asked, "Can you go to the grocery store for me?"

"Sure. Make me a list. I have some last minute shopping to do. I'll swing by there on my way home."

"You'll have to go to Big Bear because Kroger's doesn't carry what I need tonight. Don't forget to pick up some eggnog, not the low-fat kind. Matt's out visiting friends but said he'd be home around three so you guys can pick out a tree at the farmer's market. You'll need time to decorate it before guests arrive," I barked out like a drill sergeant facing new recruits.

"Not to worry; I'll be back by then." He grabbed his plastic mug, pocketed the list, pecked my cheek, and left.

Matt returned around 2:00 p.m., fixed a sandwich, and began to watch TV.

I called to him from the kitchen.

"Guess what's on? *It's a Wonderful Life*. They play it nonstop on Christmas Eve. Terry will want all of us to watch it together." I emptied the dishwasher and polished the silver.

Later, while preparing a cup of herbal tea, I glanced at the kitchen clock: 3:30 p.m.

Where the heck is he?

My good angel whispered.

He's late because the grocery store is mobbed with holiday shoppers.

Her suspicious sister interrupted.

Yeah, sure. You're only fooling yourself. You know what he's up to.

4:00 p.m., no call.

"Mom, I'd better get to the farmer's market to pick out a tree if you want to decorate it before the party tonight."

"I hate that you and Terry can't go together, especially this year. You've been picking out the perfect tree together for what ten, fifteen years? But you're right. We can't wait. Better get going. Drive carefully."

He patted me on the back.

"Don't worry, Mom, he's probably at the mall doing some last minute shopping and got stuck in traffic."

5:00 p.m., no phone call.

At 5:30 p.m., Terry rushed into the kitchen.

Instead of a bundle of groceries, he carried in a bag full of lies.

"Frannie, you aren't going to believe this. I was at Brown's Feed and Seed picking up a dog door so I can finally install it for you for Christmas. I get to the parking lot and laid the package on the fender of the truck beside me. Barely brushed against it. From out of nowhere these two hillbillies start yelling at me for messing up their truck. I apologized, but they kept at it. Screamed like cats stuffed in a laundry bag. I tried to ignore them and got in the car. When I left the parking lot, they pulled out behind, followed me and tried to cut me off. Now get this, their truck rammed into my back fender. They gave me the finger and drove off before I could get their license plate number."

"What? Are you okay? Is the car badly damaged? Did you call the police? Why didn't you call me?"

"Don't worry. Simply a little fender-bender. Not much damage. Not enough to call the police or the insurance company. I'll take it to a body shop next week to have it fixed"

My radar slammed in. Finally. My good angel shouted, *Stay calm!*

"So did you get to the grocery store?"

"Well, here's the thing. After all that, I drove to Big Bear and it was mobbed. It took me a while to get the items on your list because I don't know my way around that store. But anyway, I left the cart at the end of an aisle while I went to look for club soda and ginger ale, and, you're not going to believe this, when I came back, the cart was gone. Nothing. Nada. I couldn't find it anywhere. I walked up and down the aisles for at least fifteen minutes. The manager even helped me look. He thought that maybe someone walked away with my cart instead of theirs and checked out with my groceries. You can't believe how crazy that place is today."

The lid above my right eye began to twitch, but my voice remained calm.

"I can understand how someone could mistake your cart for theirs. It happened to me once. But I can't understand how anyone wouldn't recognize the mistake at the checkout counter."

"You would think so. I swear to you that I searched every inch of that store *and* the parking lot and couldn't find the cart."

"Well, it didn't simply disappear like Houdini or something."

"It's a true bafflement, Frannie. A true bafflement."

Even then, I wasn't entirely sure that Terry had suffered another blackout. More likely, I didn't want to believe it. He fabricated the hillbilly, missing grocery cart story to cover up for the fender-bender. To keep the peace, I swallowed his lie. I didn't want to argue and upset Matt. And it was too late to cancel our open house.

"Why don't you take a hot shower and a nap before our company gets here? Everything's under control. Matt's going to set up the tree and we'll decorate it while you sleep." While Terry showered, I wrote out a list of items we needed for the party and sent Matt to the grocery store

I was confident that after a nap, Terry would perk up, play host, and make jolly. Like a seasoned soldier, I had become a pro at damage control. But during the last year, Terry's binges and blackouts had escalated. Riding one tumultuous wave after another, I strained to keep afloat and paddle into calm water. Although caught in a riptide, I wasn't prepared to drown.

Several days earlier, we had met for dinner at the Farm Table Restaurant and ordered our usual: beans and corn bread with a side of slaw. I rattled on about Christmas gifts and plans for our open house. "I am so excited that Matt's coming home. I can't wait to pick him up at the airport." Terry seemed distracted and fiddled with his jacket pockets. When we were about to leave, he couldn't find his car keys. "Are you sure you don't have them? Look again. Try your pants pockets. Maybe you locked them in the car?"

"I don't know," he whispered, avoiding my eyes. "Can't remember."

"I think I might have one of your car keys in my glove compartment. Wait here. My car's across the street."

I returned with a key to his car. "Boy, did we get lucky. So where did you park your car?"

He looked away. "I don't know."

"Are you telling me that you don't know where you parked your car?"

Terry had no answer.

I drove my Protégé around the four square block radius of downtown South Charleston. No car.

"I'm exhausted. Let's go home. We can come back tomorrow and search for it in the daylight." We drove home without a word. The next day Terry caught a ride to work with a friend;

that evening he arrived home with his car. The front fender was badly dented.

Nothing was said.

In the aftermath of Terry's blackouts, I either acted like the Grand Inquisitor, (which was futile because he could not remember anything that had happened) or a cloistered nun who'd taken a vow of silence. Silence was superior to screaming. Although not always successfully, I worked hard to control my fiery Italian temper, especially that week before Christmas.

While Terry preferred to socialize in smaller groups, he had always been a gracious host at our crowded annual open house. He always pitched in to help me prepare. Sometimes, he'd hover around like a doting mother preparing her child for the first day of school.

"Do you think we have enough ice?" he'd ask. "I could run to the Go-Mart and pick up a big bag. What about soft drinks or beer?"

"We have plenty of ice and drinks. Besides, people will bring a six-pack or bottle of wine. Relax. I have it under control. Why don't you walk the dog, read a book, watch TV, or something?"

But this Christmas Eve, he slept. Matt and I decorated the tree. With a forced cheerfulness, we unpacked cherished ornaments wrapped in tissue paper: the petrified marshmallow sprinkled with specks of red glitter and held together with toothpicks that Matt had crafted in kindergarten; the shiny gray-and-blue ball with the Dallas Cowboys logo; the metal cactus from Terry's cousin Dinah in Dallas with a tarnished angel from my mother topping the highest branch; and a replica of the Empire State Building from my sister. Each year, Terry fumbled to untangle strings of white lights and arrange them on the tree. "That looks good," I'd say, "but you need to cover some of the branches on the back of the tree. It looks a little bare back there. And that string in the front by the candy cane needs to be moved a little to the right."

"Frannie, Jeez, you're so particular."

I guess "particular" could be another word for "controlling." I see that now, but then I wanted everything to look nice, especially at Christmas.

This year, Matt strung solo. After we filled the tree with ornaments, Matt climbed on a stepladder to place the angel on top. Then we darkened the room and plugged in the lights. Our perfect tree stood resplendent in the great room under a vaulted ceiling in front of a large picture window, like those "home for the holidays" ads in the L.L. Bean catalog. Ten months earlier, when a realtor had showed us the house for the first time, I'd envisioned a magnificent Christmas tree sitting in that exact spot. Matt and I placed many gifts at the base of the tree.

"Seems like we have more and more each year, Mom."

"Well, it's a special year. We're in our new home and you're with us. It's a blessing that we're all together."

While I put out the silverware and glasses on the dining room table, Terry finally woke up from his nap and showered. After a hot bath, I dressed in black slacks, a red turtleneck, my Christmas cardigan with red and green wreaths and silver bells, and a pair of sterling silver angel earrings, a present from Terry the Christmas before. Then I sprayed my neck and wrists with cologne, a gift from Terry's mom. When I walked into the living room to ask Terry to fasten a bracelet for me, he was slumped in his Lazy Boy chair. He wore a clean pair of jeans, a denim shirt, and a green and red cardigan sweater. At that point, Matt bounced in with my camera.

"Come on, you guys, stand in front of the tree so I can get a few pictures." Terry pulled himself up and I followed. He stood stiffly, with only a hint of a smile, his glazed eyes looking directly into the camera. In another shot, he draped his arm around my right shoulder, as our lips twisted into tight smiles.

The early guests arrived. Terry remained fixed in his chair. At one point he staggered into the kitchen and managed to make it back to his chair without creating a scene. *Christ, why tonight?* I thought. *He always picks the worst times to get drunk!*

Friends and neighbors filed in and out, like passengers at a crowded airport terminal. Some were making the rounds of holiday parties; others left for midnight church services. As I circulated, I fixed my radar on Terry. He sat alone while guests maneuvered around him with the tact of seasoned diplomats. As I refilled glasses, replenished food, and chatted, I calculated how best to stir this creature from the living room to our bedroom on this night before Christmas.

And then it happened.

Terry lurched upright. He wobbled from his chair toward the dining-room table, picked up a clear plastic cup, and poured himself a glass of white wine. I watched him, unbelieving, transfixed. He lifted the bottle, poured the wine, brought the cup to his lips, and drank—as deliberately as a priest on the altar during my Catholic girlhood, or as if he were an actor on stage, illuminated by a spotlight's glare.

Did that happen? Did he actually drink that wine, right in front of me?

Since returning from the treatment center, Terry had never drunk alcohol in front of me. That's not to say that he didn't drink. That's not to say that he didn't hide his booze all over the house. That's not to say that we didn't argue regularly over his drinking. That's not to say that our marriage wasn't upended by the tidal wave of his addiction to alcohol. But, during all of those later years, we'd held fast to one unspoken agreement: Under no circumstances would Terry drink in front of me. And if he didn't drink in front of me, well, then maybe, he wasn't drinking at all.

Our denial had fueled this charade for years.

I deeply regret that when Terry returned from the treatment center that I didn't insist we would not have any liquor in our home. I could have easily forgone an occasional glass of wine. But Terry assured me that having wine and beer in our house would not be a problem. Besides, I reasoned that alcohol was readily available outside our home, so it didn't much matter if I drank a glass of wine at dinner. Yet, I should not have asked more of my husband than I was willing to do myself.

Plastic cup still in hand, Terry stumbled across the room and sank back into his chair. I caught our friend Jay's eye and nodded toward Terry. I walked over, knelt beside him and whispered: "Looks as if you aren't feeling well. I'm going to help you to bed." Jay followed me. We positioned Terry's bulky body between us, lifted an arm over each of our shoulders and navigated around clusters of guests. Terry collapsed on top of the bed. I removed his shoes, covered him with a quilt and returned to our guests.

"Terry seems to have come down with a touch of the flu. He took a prescription pill earlier this evening and it must have knocked him out." No one responded. Our good friends had heard this tale before. After a few awkward moments, someone turned on the CD player. We sang Christmas carols until the last guest left after midnight.

I cleared the table, rinsed the crystal and china, piled trays, platters, cups, silverware, and napkins on the kitchen counter, and then crawled into bed without shedding my clothes, washing my face, or brushing my teeth. Terry's heavy snores coupled with my despair kept me awake. After an hour of tossing and turning, I popped a Valium and dragged myself to the guest room where I read a copy of *Newsweek* until I drifted off.

That year we never got around to watching *It's a Wonderful Life*. Like George Bailey, we needed a miracle to save us. But none was forthcoming.

DARK WINE WATERS

CHAPTER TWELVE

Tsunami

Hope is the last thing we lose.

Italian proverb

After a restless night, I found Terry seated in his Lazy Boy, exactly like the night before. It was 10:00 a.m. The Christmas tree stood behind his chair. Red, silver, and green ornaments sparkled under the slanting rays of light. Terry's left hand trembled slightly as he lowered his plastic mug to the floor. His vacant eyes stared ahead.

"Good morning," I said. Slight nod, but no other response. "How do you like the tree? Don't you think Matt and I did a good job?" Still no response, "Look, I'm going to wash up and make some coffee. I was up pretty late last night washing crystal and china. We have a busy day ahead. I'll be back in a few minutes."

As I carried my steaming mug and sat on the sofa opposite him, I thought, *stay calm.*

"Don't we have a ton of gifts this year? We always say we're going to cut down, but we never do. Guess we went overboard because Matt's back home. Oh well, 'tis the season" I said, feigning good cheer. Then I cleared my throat.

"Um, we need to talk about last night. I hope we can clear the air before Matt gets up."

Terry sipped from his cup and faced me.

"Frannie, I'm sorry. What can I say? Looks like I may have surpassed my limit for messing up this time."

Unable to suppress the words, I shot back, "Terry, you surpassed your limit a long time ago," my voice trembling with a mixture of anger and sarcasm. He glanced down at his hands. I looked out the window and circled the rim of the mug with my index finger. We sat still for the next few minutes. Then, I started the rationalizing, guilt-tripping, playing martyr, and controlling; unpacking most of the tools of the codependent's thankless trade:

"Look, it's Christmas. Matt's home for such a short time. I want him to have a happy holiday, even if we have to pretend . . ." Pretending; codependents are as good at pretending as addicts are. I went on.

"I think we should go ahead with our plans for today. Open our gifts this morning, have a bite to eat, and then get ready to go to Rhonda's. She's expecting us around three." The desire to save face; another trick in the codependent's book.

"Since I made two trays of lasagna and two dozen meatballs, we can't very well not show up. I'm not going to push you, but I'd certainly like for the three of us to go together." That slight hint of martyrdom: "I'm not going to push you." And now for the big finish: a kindly gesture.

"Why don't you rest for a while and then take a shower? You'll feel better. I don't want to get into a big thing this morning, so I'm getting dressed and then going for a walk. Matt should be up when I get back. Then we can open our presents."

These codependent behaviors are easy to identify now. Hindsight surely is twenty-twenty. Back then, I couldn't see.

I threw on heavy sweats, grabbed my parka, hat, and mittens and slammed the back door. Cold air hit me as I climbed the steep hill in front of our house and walked the mile-long loop around the neighborhood. Tall, bare trees framed the well maintained split-level houses on either side of the road. As I passed lampposts decorated with bright red bows and doors hung with stately wreaths, my body felt as tightly coiled as the wires on strings of Christmas lights. I envied families opening presents around their respective hearths, those Norman Rockwell scenes and "I'll Be Home for Christmas" Kodak commercials. Like the Capra movie, these images played nonstop from Thanksgiving until New Year's Day. Though Terry warmed to the holiday spirit, he felt that the holidays were overrated. "Too much hype and too many expectations. Actually, a whole bunch of people get depressed."

As I made my way around the neighborhood, my thoughts spun around in my brain. *Why does he always pick the worst times to get drunk? Why do I continue to put up with this? What if the blackouts get worse? How are we going to get through today? Should we go to Rhonda's or should I call with an excuse? I have a cold, Terry has the flu, the electricity went out, or our roof sprung a leak. Or should I be honest and say, 'Rhonda, I am suffering from that worst of all maladies: a broken heart.' She'd understand.*

I mentally unwrapped my Christmas "pity" packages and headed toward home. I've since learned ways to circumvent my "pity parties." I'm not always successful.

When I returned, Terry's Taurus wasn't in the driveway. *Good,* I thought, *we'll both have time to cool down.*

I cleaned the kitchen mess, then showered and dressed.

I returned to the living room with another mug of coffee.

I sat on the couch.

Our carefully wrapped gifts were piled high on the hearth. Years before, I'd purchased a six-foot-long, red-and-white striped stocking for Terry. Each Christmas when Matt and I hung our stockings, we teased him. "Santa Claus will get a hernia hauling stuffers just for your stocking." Now his stocking lay on the hearth, neatly folded, with a yellow post-it note on top that read, "Thanks, Terry." Beside his stocking lay an expensive cigar, a box of paper clips, a pair of wool socks, a package of jockey shorts, a bag of pistachio nuts, a Toblerone chocolate bar, a new deck of playing cards, golf balls with the Dallas Cowboys imprint, ballpoint pens, and razor blades.

Since he often left to lick his wounds during a hangover, I expected that he'd return later that day. We'd salvage Christmas: open the presents, have a snack, and drive to Rhonda's for her holiday gathering. Like combat veterans during war, Terry and I would declare a twenty-four hour truce. In a few days, we'd pack the episode away with our presents and decorations and move on. Terry would vow to try harder; I'd vow to be more patient. And we'd jump back into therapy. A new year, a fresh start, clear sailing ahead. This holiday drama would wash away and we'd settle back into our day-to-day routine. Maybe we could visit Matt when he returned to Europe.

After twenty years our performances were flawless: binge, argue, make-up, bounce back; binge, argue, make-up, bounce back. From turbulence to tranquility and back again. Strong emotions cresting in high tides and fading in low ones. The insidious addiction cycle. Because Terry functioned well between binges, I harbored false hope. Besides, this upcoming new round of marital therapy was my insurance that we would avoid a disaster.

But during the past year, the binges had cycled quickly, with fewer abstinent interludes. Still we got by. My panic attacks returned, but they were controllable, with medication prescribed by my psychiatrist. Best I could tell, Terry performed well at work. In fact, he'd taken on a consulting job to make extra money. Granted, he hadn't helped much with the Christmas preparations. Then again, he had spent hours trying to install a doggie door in the garage, since we planned to expand our family with a puppy from the pound.

Wearing his bathrobe, Matt had wandered into the living room sometime during my reverie.

"Mom, when are we going to open the gifts?"

"Let's wait for Terry to get back."

"Where did he go?"

"I think he may have gone for ice at the 7-Eleven."

I knew that Matt suspected otherwise, but I said nothing.

We waited. I wrapped a few presents to take to Rhonda's and fiddled around in the kitchen. Matt watched a ballgame on TV. By 2:00 p.m. Terry hadn't returned. *What should I do? Should I stay home and wait for him? Should Matt and I head for Rhonda's?* Although I didn't feel like socializing, I'd prepared trays of food. Matt wanted to get together with old friends who'd be there. I didn't want to worry him. *Better to go than wait around for Terry to show up.*

"Let's get ready to go. We'll open presents later, when Terry gets home." I penciled a note for Terry. Then Matt and I carried a crockpot of meatballs, two trays of lasagna, and presents to the trunk of my Protégé.

Rhonda's house was located deep in the woods. "Bumpy ride, Mom," Matt said, as we drove five miles on a rutted road. "Do you ever think they're going to fix the road out here?"

"Haven't since I've known them. And that's been a pretty long time."

The mood at Rhonda's was festive.

"Hey, here's the lasagna and meatballs," someone called out as we hung our coats on pegs in the mud room. A ten-foot tree replete with hundreds of tiny white lights sparkled in the middle of the enormous living room. The dining room table, covered with a white linen tablecloth, was filled with homemade breads, salads, vegetables, fruit, and cheese trays. Cookies, cakes, pies, and fudge sat on an antique sideboard. Bottles of wine, Perrier, and soft drinks covered the kitchen table.

Rhonda greeted me with a hug, "Oh, I'm so glad you and Matt could come. Where's Terry?"

"Oh, he's in the middle of a mega-allergy attack. He's probably allergic to the Christmas tree. Sneezing and wheezing like crazy. You know how he is, allergic to almost everything. He's genuinely disappointed that he couldn't be here and sends his love."

"Oh, I'm so sorry. Maybe he can drive out later. Can I get you a glass of wine? Where's Matt? I can't wait to see him."

I knew Rhonda knew that I was lying. Thankfully nothing more was said. Like a master chef, I folded lies into lies, concocting a soufflé flavored with equal parts denial and the delusion that we were in control of our lives. The addiction experts label this "mental mismanagement." Though the evidence was as solid as a sheet of steel, we wouldn't admit that our lives were out of control. We were as sick as our lies.

And so I once again covered for Terry. After all, I couldn't blurt out the truth. *My husband's hung over again. Last week, he couldn't find his car. Yesterday, he had a fender bender and blacked out in the middle of Big Bear. Came up with some cockamamie story about hillbillies and a stolen grocery cart. He drove home, even though he had no business driving in his condition. Wait. There's more. Last night at our open house, he took a drink right in front of me. Later he collapsed in bed. I was so embarrassed. This morning he left the house without a word. I haven't heard from him all day. He's probably perched on a bar stool in some hotel downtown right now.*

I envied Rhonda's other friends, talking, laughing, exchanging gossip and gifts. *Why can't we be normal like them? Do they pity me? Do they pity us? Do I pity myself?*

Matt and I left early and joked about how everyone loved my lasagna and meatballs. "Mom, all I got was a tiny piece of the veggie lasagna and one lousy meatball."

"Not to worry, honey. I'll cook up another batch before you leave."

Terry's car wasn't parked in the driveway when we arrived home at 8:00 p.m. I raced to the telephone answering machine. It blinked "00." I changed into flannel pajamas, brewed tea, and stretched out on the couch in front of the hearth. Matt left to visit with an old high school friend.

"You going to be okay, Mom? You want me to stay and wait around?"

"No, you go. I'm fine."

Too weary to light a fire, I sat in the shadow of a dim hallway light and stared at our unopened presents, wrapped in paper festooned with jolly Santas and snowmen and trimmed with red and green ribbons and bows.

No call. At ten o'clock, I phoned our friend Jay. He'd witnessed the scene the night before and had helped ease Terry into the bedroom.

"Listen, this may be premature, and I hesitated calling. But I'm worried. Terry left the house around eleven o'clock this morning and I haven't heard from him since. Matt and I waited for him to open presents, but he didn't show. We left for Rhonda's house about two in the afternoon. I figured he'd be home when we got back. But he still hasn't shown up. There were no messages on the answering machine. That's not like him. I'm thinking of calling the hospitals."

"Has he done this before? Not phoned?"

"He's left before. Usually comes dragging in late. But he always phones to let me know that he's okay. Even when he's in pretty bad shape, he phones."

"How long has he been gone?"

"What time is it now? I went for a walk around eleven this morning, and he wasn't home when I returned. So about twelve hours."

"I don't think there's anything to worry about. He'll probably come home later after you're asleep. Besides, you can't report a missing person for at least twenty-four hours, though I doubt that he's missing. Don't worry. Get some sleep. He'll be back later tonight."

"Okay, you're probably right."

I went to bed but couldn't sleep, so I read a copy of *Newsweek*. Around two, I finally drifted off.

I awoke some hours later; but still early in the morning.

Terry wasn't in bed beside me. I slipped into my robe and a pair of clogs, grabbed the morning paper outside the front door, and walked to the driveway. The Taurus wasn't parked there. Terry hadn't phoned. Matt appeared in his bathrobe about 10:00 a.m.

"Mom, did Terry come home last night and sleep it off?"

"Honey, he still isn't here. But I'm sure that he'll call us soon. Might as well have some breakfast." I set English muffins and orange juice on the dining room table where they kept company with a holly-and-pinecone centerpiece. While we ate, I tuned in to public radio to fill the silence.

After breakfast, Matt said, "Well, Mom, do you think we should open our gifts and save Terry's for later when he comes back?"

"That sounds like a good plan."

And so we revised our Christmas morning ritual from years past, when we would sit around the hearth sipping coffee, and Terry and Matt drank Diet Coke and munched on homemade cinnamon rolls. Matt would sort through the gifts piled under the tree and place a pile beside each of us. We took turns opening each gift and commented on whose pile was the biggest. "Matt, it definitely looks like this year you got the most," Terry would tease. After admiring each gift, we'd empty the stockings, including those with treats for our cat, Oreo, and our shepherd, Lucky. Then we'd toss wrapping paper, bows, and empty boxes into plastic bags, after which Terry would prepare his traditional brunch.

Instead, that morning-after Christmas, Matt sorted the gifts into piles. He placed Terry's at the foot of his recliner. I feigned enthusiasm to mask the tension as we opened each gift. For me, a handmade jewelry box and a prayer rug that Matt had purchased in Morocco.

"It's lovely, honey. So exotic. I'll treasure it."

For Matt, an electronic organizer, travel alarm, a poncho, and a navy fleece jacket from a well-known retailer. Our gift exchange was quick and quiet. We didn't mention Terry, though his unopened gifts spoke volumes.

Matt had arranged to visit a friend that afternoon.

"I'm supposed to go over to Denny's to watch a game with some of the guys. But I can stay here with you."

"Don't be silly. Of course, you should go. All of your friends are dying to see you. I'm okay. I am. Terry's bound to show up anytime soon."

"Are you sure? You have Denny's phone number if you need me. Make sure you call me as soon as Terry gets home."

To keep busy I cleaned the refrigerator and then placed a phone call to Jay. "Have you heard anything?" I asked. "No, but don't worry, he'll turn up and I'll call you if I hear from him."

Next, I contacted admissions at the local hospitals. No Terry. I thought about contacting the police, but what would I say? *I'm sorry to bother you, but my husband's been missing since yesterday morning after we argued over his getting drunk on Christmas Eve. He didn't show up for Christmas yesterday, isn't at work today, and I don't know where the hell he is.* Characters in TV shows, like "Law and Order," make statements like that. I don't. I don't report missing persons. And after years of binges and blackouts, I don't panic anymore. *He'll call,* I assured myself. *He'll come back. He always does.*

I checked in with Jay again.

"Fran, wait a while and try not to worry. He's bound to show up. And let me know as soon as he gets there."

Nine o'clock that evening, still no call.

I sipped a cup of tea in front of the low light of a fire and stared at Terry's unopened presents piled on the hearth. *What now?* I thought. My husband had been missing well over twenty-four hours. My mind swung from desperation to hope and back again. *Maybe he's been in a car crash, bleeding in a ditch on a God-forsaken country road, alone and helpless in the pitch-black cold. No, don't overreact. He's probably too ashamed to come home. Maybe he crashed at a motel to sleep it off. Or he went to a movie. But even when he's barely able to function, he phones to check in. He always phones.*

Two months earlier, after a binge, I had screamed. "We're heading toward a crisis, and I don't know how to stop it."

Calmly, he had replied, "Frannie, you over-dramatize everything. It's no big deal. I'm doing fine. You know I love you. Everything's going to be fine." Exhausted from another outburst, I'd walked away. Later that evening, he sat on the edge of the bed and caressed my hand. "I'm sorry. I love you." He stroked the nape of my neck and drew me toward him. We made love. In the afterglow, everything was fine, like he promised.

Except, it wasn't.

I thought about phoning Matt, but decided against it. He'd been away for the past year and his time home was limited. Best for him to enjoy his friends.

Think logically, think rationally. There's a reason that he hasn't come home. Please, God, help me. What should I do? I can't sit here and do nothing. But what can I do? Adrenaline shot through every cell of my body. I craved a cigarette. I could have smoked a carton.

Earlier that day, I'd placed three phone calls to Terry's office. He wasn't there. "If he does come in, have him call me immediately. It's extremely important," I said to the secretary in a voice as calm as a gambler bluffing a winning hand. When Terry had introduced me to poker, he'd said, "Stay cool and play your cards close to the chest." *Stay cool*, I thought, *try to stay cool.*

Should I call friends and Terry's coworkers to ask if they've seen or heard from him? If I call them, do I tell the truth or lie? Do I blurt out my fears? What if they tell me to call the police? Calling the police means this is serious. This can't be that serious. He's pulled this before. Well, not for this long. Yes, but he always shows up or at least calls. Why hasn't he called? It's not like him to not call. I stuck my hands behind my back and rubbed them together. I twisted my neck back and forth to unlock tense muscles. I rubbed my forehead. I sucked my breath; *in, out, release, in, out, release. Deep, deep breath. Stay cool. Don't overreact. He'll call. Wait, simply wait.*

I brewed a cup of herbal tea and slumped on the sofa facing the hearth and stared at Terry's unopened presents. I had bought him a new light-blue cashmere sweater from a pricey catalog because the old one had moth holes. I knew he'd like it, but he'd admonish me for spending too much money.

"Frannie, the old one's fine." The other gifts were much less lavish, white crew socks, a few paperback mysteries, and a terrycloth bathrobe. I walked over to the hearth and ran my hand over the box that held the sweater.

In that moment, emotion trumped logic. The ice-in-my-stomach sensation flooded me. I whispered, "He's dead." Nothing short of Terry walking through our front door would have convinced me otherwise.

Like a dying patient, I bargained for a miracle. *Please, God, let him be alive. Please, help me not to get carried away with this, not to* panic and overreact. *After all, I don't know anything for sure. God, help me find Terry and let him be alive.*

I remembered one night when Matt was a teenager and hadn't come home or called by 4:00 a.m. I'd visualized his broken body pinned beneath a steering wheel, windshield shattered, metal twisted, tires blown from the impact of a head-on collision. And I'd been wrong, that time. I clung to that for as long as I could.

Around ten o'clock, I called Jay.

"It's Fran. Terry wasn't at work and hasn't called. I phoned the hospitals and he wasn't at any of them. He's been missing now for over twenty-four hours. Something's wrong. I'm seriously scared."

"Mindy and I will be there in ten minutes." That's all he said.

Every detail of the events that followed is imprinted in my memory in indelible ink.

Months later, I recorded them in my journal:

I remember the cold and darkness. Wind blowing across the dark, silent river. We found his Taurus in the deserted parking lot of the Union Building. It was locked. Then a delivery man entered Terry's office building, and we followed like robots. Rode up a noisy elevator in silence. Faint light from one fluorescent bulb at the landing. Jay walked down the hall and opened the door to Terry's messy office. "No one in here." He took my hand. We walked slowly up and down the long corridor, checking doors that were locked. Then Jay opened the door to the law library. I stood directly behind him but was able to catch just a glimpse of Terry lying face down on the floor, a black plastic bag over his head. I screamed. Jay shoved me away from the door into the hall. I leaned against a wall and sank to the floor. Jay closed the door gently and knelt beside me. He rocked me back and forth, repeating, "It's not your fault. It's not your fault," over and over. Suddenly, bright lights, flashbulbs, policemen, questions, phone calls, and a gurney on wheels. Terry's body covered with a sheet. I felt nauseated, numb . . . confused, thoughts jumbled, mouth mute, heart frozen and locked in unspeakable pain. This can't be real. How can this be real? In silence, Terry rode down that noisy elevator for the last time. In silence. Eternal silence.

The rest of that evening was blank. I don't recall leaving the office building, driving home, or sleeping. But I'll never forget that millisecond when I caught a glimpse of my husband's dead body, face down, sprawled on a gray rug, wearing his faded jeans, green and red sweater, gray windbreaker, scuffed sneakers, with his tattered leather bag by his side. And that black trash bag pulled tight over his face like an executioner's mask.

PART IV

Healing Water Recovery

RECOGNIZING THAT WE ARE POWERLESS AND BECOMING

WILLING TO SURRENDER ARE THE FIRST STEPS IN THE

JOURNEY TOWARD RESTORING OUR LIVES.

DARK WINE WATERS

CHAPTER THIRTEEN

Empty Vessel

Earth has no sorrow that heaven cannot heal.

Thomas More

I can't recall whether or not I slept or ate after discovering Terry's corpse. But I do recall that shock waves propelled me into action. When I broke the news to Matt the following morning, he asked, "Why? Mom, why did he do this to us?" I didn't have an answer. I contacted the funeral home where Jay had arranged his mother's wake the previous year. I requested a cremation as quickly as possible.

"We can't do it here, but we can make arrangements at the crematorium in Beckley," the director informed me. "I can arrange it for you within the next two days."

I knew that Terry did not want his body embalmed and displayed in an open casket. Toward the end of his life, not only was my husband's spirit broken, but his body was ravaged. Somewhere I'd read that Eastern teachers believe that cremation helps the dead recognize immediately that the body is an illusion that has little to do with someone's true nature. I took comfort in that.

I recalled our conversation about cremation at Holden Beach the summer before.

"No casket, no funeral, no frills. No fancy clothes, embalming, and lipstick. My mom won't object since she had Rex cremated. He was the first in my family. Most of them were okay with it, but I'm sure a few of the militant Baptists raised their eyebrows."

But the day before my husband's body was to be transported to Beckley, I panicked. I remember reading in the *Tibetan Book of the Dead* that consciousness lasts for three days. Terry needed time to pass over, and I wasn't ready to let him go. I had caught only a glimpse of his dead body. I hadn't touched him. I hadn't talked to him. I hadn't said goodbye. I phoned the funeral director.

"Please help. I must change some of the arrangements that I made yesterday. I want to spend some time with my husband before the cremation."

"We were planning to move his body today. But I think I can delay it. We can arrange to place him on a portable bed in a small room off the chapel tomorrow morning. Would that be agreeable to you?"

"Yes, fine, thank you."

I gathered clean clothing: underwear and socks, a pair of Dockers, a denim shirt, a pair of loafers, and his brown felt Indiana-Jones hat. No suit, tie, or jewelry. I ironed the pants and shirt, folded them carefully and placed everything in a shopping bag. Matt offered to deliver them to the funeral home.

"And what else can I do, Mom? What else can I do for you?"

I asked him to phone close friends. "Tell them that Terry's body will be at the funeral home from 9:00 a.m. to noon tomorrow. Invite them to come. If they don't feel comfortable, tell them I'll understand and I'll see them later on."

Early the next morning I carried a large wicker basket to the funeral parlor, filled with carefully chosen icons: a worn quilt that had belonged to Terry's grandmother, my mother's clear glass rosary beads, a small stuffed bear, a sand dollar from Holden Beach, a rock from our garden, a fresh yellow rose, a lotto ticket, a golf ball, a cigar, a deck of cards, and a pink candle. I dug out one of Terry's prized possessions, a baseball autographed by members of the 1957 Boston Red Sox team, Ted Williams, Frank Malzone, Jim Piersall, and Frank Sullivan. I gathered several books, a Bible, Stephen Levine's book, *Who Dies?* Terry's copy of *Zen Flesh, Zen Bones* with the purchase price of $1.47 stamped on the inside cover. Finally, I selected a few photos: one of Matt, Terry, and me at Holden Beach, another of our beloved German Shepherd, Lucky, and a black-and-white of his mother and father while they were courting. I could almost hear him say: "Frannie, you never pack light." Why change now?

Matt drove me to the funeral home, but decided not to spend time with Terry's body. "Mom, I honestly can't do it. I want to remember him alive."

"That's fine, honey, whatever you want to do."

"I'll wait here in case some of your friends stop by."

"Thanks." I hugged him tight and then entered the tiny room lit by one red votive candle. First, I covered him with his grandmother's quilt and arranged the rosary beads, yellow rose and sand dollar on his chest. I placed his Indiana Jones hat over his folded hands. I arranged the teddy bear, golf ball, lotto ticket, rock, cigar, deck of cards, baseball, and photos in two rows, one on each side of his body. Those familiar objects might ease his journey into the unknown. Then I lit the pink candle and tried to pray, but I couldn't focus. Like a discarded rag doll, I sank into a red velvet chair in one corner and sobbed. Eventually, I inched forward and knelt next to his body. I placed his hand in mine. It was cold and stiff, so unlike the warm, gentle hands that had reached out to me a thousand times, the hands that massaged my feet, sponged my back, caressed my breasts, rubbed my thighs, scratched my back, smoothed my hair, and wiped away my tears. The hand that I held as we walked along the shore encircled in sunlight at Holden Beach only six months before.

I selected short excerpts to read. Stephen Levine's "A Guided Death Transition Meditation," urged the deceased to embrace the transition from life to death, to dissolve into clear light, to be open, to let go. From *Zen Flesh, Zen Bones* I read a passage about truth and the "path of no coming and no going."

I ended with the "Prayer to Saint Francis," my patron saint.

> "Lord make me an instrument of Thy peace. Where there is hatred, let me sow love; where there is injury, pardon; where there is doubt, faith; where there is despair, hope; where there is darkness, light; and where there is sadness, joy.

> "O, Divine Master, grant that I may not so much seek to be consoled, as to console; to be understood as to understand; to be loved, as to love; for it is in giving that we receive; it is pardoning that we are pardoned, and it is in dying that we are born to eternal life."

Then I spoke to Terry, as I'd done thousands of times during our twenty years together.

"Why did you leave me? What am I going to do without you? Why did you do it? What did you think in those final moments? Did you think of me? Did you think of Matt? Did you think of anything at all?" (I imagined a wink and hearing him say, "You ask too many questions.")

"How could this have happened? We talked about returning to Italy, maybe next summer. You said you wanted to stay at the Hotel Splendide in Bellagio, retrace our steps, a second honeymoon. And what about your birthday note to me? It was so tender and full of hope. Your birthday was only three weeks ago. What happened?

"And your mother? She screamed when I told her the news. I waited to phone her as long as I could; I dreaded making that call. She was devastated. And so was the rest of your family in Dallas. All those years you hid from her. All those years she refused to believe that you had a drinking problem. Never suspected. 'He was perfect,' she said to me. 'Perfect.'"

During that grief-stricken phone call, Zinna recalled our recent Thanksgiving visit when Terry drove to Lowe's to purchase a floor lamp and a spotlight for the garage door. Back at the house, he assembled the lamp and replaced the light. Then he spread several bags of mulch over Zinna's flower beds in the back yard.

"Only a few weeks ago, he was fine. He was fine when he was here. He did all those chores around the house. We had such a nice visit. We went to El Fenix, like we always did. How could this happen? I can't understand. I simply can't understand."

Even though his dead body lay a foot in front of me, I couldn't understand either. *How could someone kill himself? And how could it be that I'd never again hear his voice or hold his hand? That we'd never make love, or catch a Saturday matinee, or cook a fine meal together, or walk in the woods, or bodysurf among the waves at Holden Beach? How could it be that he'd never hold me in his arms, or make me laugh, or wipe away my tears?*

I moved across the room, sat beside his body and cried. I closed my eyes and took deep breaths. *Follow your breath, think of your breath, deep, deep, in, out, in, out, come back to your breath. Slow, take it slow.* I knelt beside him and whispered: "Let go, let go, don't hold back, leave that broken body. Forgive yourself, free yourself, don't look back, just head toward the light. You don't have to struggle anymore. The pain is gone. You can rest now. All your sorrows, so many sorrows, gone. They're gone." I stroked his right cheek, kissed his bloodless lips, removed his hat, and left the room.

Matt and several close friends were gathered in the hallway talking quietly. Matt put his arm around my shoulder.

"Mom, I still can't go in there. Is that all right?"

"Yes. It's fine. You've been a big comfort to me. Don't upset yourself over not wanting to view Terry's body." A few friends entered to pay respects, others simply stayed with me. We hugged, we cried, we spoke in whispers so as not to disturb the spirits who gathered to transport his soul.

That afternoon, friends and neighbors came and went at the house. I sat on a bench overlooking the creek in our backyard on that warm, December day. Ginny, one of Terry's friends from college, arrived with an enormous green basket filled with fresh fruit and flowers. Mindy and Jay carried a meat-and-cheese platter. Neighbors dropped off baked goods. Food, drinks, and flowers flooded the house. Matt screened phone calls and played host.

Surrounded by all this activity, I felt like the survivor of a shipwreck trying to get my bearings. *Who is that, talking, walking, crying, and answering questions?* Waves of shock, disbelief, and grief carried me through the following week when Matt and I arranged for Terry's memorial service. I forced myself to go to the pool. Suicide was alien and dreadful; swimming was familiar and comforting. The water soothed me.

Friends pressed me for decisions I wasn't prepared to make.

"What are you going to do after the cremation?"

"Will there be a memorial service?"

"When and where?"

"Who do you want to call?"

"What about family and friends from out of state?"

"Who should be contacted at the university?"

"Will you arrange for Terry's mother to fly in?"

Though confused and indecisive, I knew this: I wanted a memorial service for Terry within the next week or so. That evening of the cremation, I sat on the couch next to Mindy.

"Well, where do you want to have the memorial service?" she asked.

"I think he would have wanted to have it here at our house, in the new wing. It isn't finished yet, but I think it'll be okay."

"Well, crowds of people will come. I'm not sure that the room will be big enough to handle the crowd. Besides where are you going to seat them? Maybe you should think about renting a room at a club or church. Maybe the funeral home."

"No. I know he'd want it here; he loved this new house, couldn't wait to have people over to show it off."

We sat in silence for a few minutes. Then she grabbed my right hand, looked me in the eye and said, "In that case, we'll have to make it work. Don't worry. We'll take care of everything. It'll work, we'll make it work."

In the next few days, she rallied our feminist friends, veterans of marches, protests, and political campaigns. Quintessential organizers, they summoned the troops to assemble tables, chairs, food, plates, cutlery, napkins, glasses, flowers, and phone calls. Even boxes of Kleenex. To my dying day, I'll bless each one of them for orchestrating Terry's West Virginia memorial service. They made it work.

DARK WINE WATERS

CHAPTER FOURTEEN

Burial at Sea

Give sorrow words, the grief that cannot speak.

W. Shakespeare, *Macbeth*

Terry was honored at three memorial services, one in the city, one in the mountains, and one at the beach. The first, a small service attended by family and a few of Zinna's neighbors, occurred at the Dickerson Chapel of the First United Methodist Church in downtown Dallas a week after he died. After any death, but particularly a sudden one, emotions run high. Sometimes long-simmering conflicts can detonate like land mines. Consider the letters that are written to advice columnists cataloging family disputes over wills, money, probate, possessions, funeral arrangements, cemeteries, and memorials. If détente isn't declared, a battle erupts with many casualties among the already bereaved.

Proper and polite southerners, members of Terry's family would never wage a full-blown battle. Their conflicts were camouflaged in talk as sweet as pralines and pecan pie. Bless their hearts. Immediately after Terry's death, his father's sister,

Aunt Frieda, phoned her minister and instructed him to "plan a memorial service much like Rex's." This preemptive strike did not sit well with Zinna. In fact, she hit the roof. Rather than confront her sister-in-law directly, she phoned to tell me that she alone would orchestrate every detail of the memorial of her only child.

Zinna resented Rex and his family. During Terry's childhood Rex had done little to support his son, either emotionally or financially. Zinna often worked two jobs to pay the mortgage on her two-bedroom bungalow. This was in the 1950s, when most women did not work outside the home. She sacrificed to meet her monthly expenses. Terry once confided that his mother didn't purchase a single new dress for eight years. She also paid Frieda to care for her son before he entered first grade. Although Terry was the center of Zinna's life, he spent much more time with his beloved "Auntie" during his formative years.

Zinna also was troubled by her sister-in-law Frieda's relationship with Rex. A veteran enabler, Frieda couldn't refuse her baby brother when he needed money and a place to crash while he sobered up. Zinna once confided, "Those Blackwells stick together no matter what."

More telling was the sisters-in-law's covert rivalry for Terry's devotion and affection. Even as a young child, he sensed an unspoken tension between them. Like a skilled mediator, he negotiated between the two cautiously. He loved them both. His aunt offered unconditional love with no strings attached. Although Zinna loved him no less, their mother-son relationship was at times uneasy. Terry felt that in his mother's eyes, he should have been "the man in the family," the unblemished hero. Her unspoken message, "Be perfect" would burden anyone, especially an intuitive, sensitive child like my husband.

During our family forays to Dallas, Terry doled out equal portions of time like a skillful waiter, always alert not to offend his mother, who handled perceived slights with "It's okay. Don't worry about me," remarks, or worse, stone silence.

"Sometimes, she acts like a martyr," he'd say, "and it makes me feel guilty."

"Oh, come on, what mother doesn't indulge in a guilt trip once in a while? It goes with the territory."

While planning her son's memorial, Zinna contacted me several times because she wanted some of the same prayers, poems, and music at both his West Virginia and Dallas services. I sent her readings and songs, which she forwarded to the minister. He finally agreed to include poems from Kahlil Gibran and Erica Jong, along with readings and prayers from the traditional liturgy. But he balked at John Lennon's "Imagine," one of my favorite songs. In fact, he flatly refused to include it. Numb from shock and grief over the suicide of her only child, Zinna became even more distraught.

However, a minor miracle occurred the evening before the service. Apparently, God Himself visited the preacher in a dream and commanded "Thou shalt include 'Imagine' in the service." (Terry would have loved the irony involved.) A fitting tribute to this child of the sixties.

I didn't attend the Texas service. Zinna sent me a copy of the eulogy given by Terry's cousin, Bobby. It included childhood memories:

> "He had two mothers—a perfect blend of Arkansas and Oklahoma. I heard 'Auntie' so often with "love" that I thought these two were synonymous. As for Zinna, I cannot correctly get Terry's inflection or his soft voice saying, "Ah, Mom," and "Um, Mom." He loved and respected her greatly."

Bobby concluded: "I did not see Terry's demons; I saw his caring nature and love for his extended family and many friends. I did not feel his pain; I felt his warmth and friendship."

Many others had also felt his warmth and friendship.

Terry's West Virginia memorial, held on January 7, was more a bittersweet "roast" than a somber service. He definitely would have enjoyed it. Some sixty friends and acquaintances gathered in our unfinished great room to share stories and memories, sing songs, (including "Imagine"), recite poetry, and watch a slide show set to music that began with Emmylou Harris's "All My Sorrows" and ended with Willy Nelson's "Sunny Side of the Street." (I was tempted to play Pearl Jam's "There He Goes," but decided against it.) Matt constructed a huge collage of twenty years' worth of family photos, many taken at Holden Beach. It sat beside the guest book.

Although I planned no formal eulogy, several close friends spoke. PC, Terry's friend for thirty years and one of the "Texas mafia" who'd settled in the mountains in the early '70s, began.

"The first time Terry landed in jail . . . ." He went on to recount several minor pranks that led to stays in the Sherman, Texas city jail during their college years. Another friend, Paul, recalled Terry slipping trick golf balls on to the tee. (He was a lousy golfer who enjoyed messing around with his buddies on the course more than the game itself.) Tyrone, a buddy from work, recalled gambling jaunts to Atlantic City, Las Vegas, and Keeneland Race Track in Kentucky, as well as Terry's record-setting, two-year win in the annual March Madness basketball tournament pool.

"He'd bet on almost anything. See that cloud out there? If he were with us today, he'd bet on how fast that cloud would move relative to the one behind it. Hell, he might even have bet on the number of people who gathered here today."

In deference to my husband, his cronies from the Thursday night poker group wore fedoras. Jay, who had discovered his dead body, reflected on Terry's unassuming nature, his empathy and compassion. Everyone laughed when he said, "Terry found the workings of household equipment to be one of life's more profound mysteries." He recalled how Terry consulted him during several mishaps with toilets that gurgled, a pilot light that turned off, then on, and then back off again, and a cranky garage door.

Their love for my husband sustained me during that time of unremitting grief. It sustains me still.

In *How Then Shall We Live*, Wayne Mueller writes that when someone dies it's comforting for loved ones to gather in a circle; their bodies touching one another helps them to feel safe And so we assembled in the backyard and joined hands in a circle. Sissy, Terry's eleven-year-old godchild, launched the first helium balloon. Seconds later an armada of bright orbs floated far above the barren trees under a clear blue sky on an unseasonably warm January 7. Someone began singing "Amazing Grace" and we all joined in, at least for the first verse.

Then we drank, laughed, toasted, snapped photos, shared memories, and shed many tears. A fitting closure for a soulful guy and a roomful of people who truly loved him.

Six months later, Terry's final memorial took place at Holden Beach on Memorial Day weekend. A private service: only me, Terry's ashes, and the ocean. As in years past, Jay and Mindy joined me at the house that we'd rented the summer before. In the subdued shadow of mourning, we fell into our familiar beach routines: long walks to the point, games of beach *bocce*, swimming, selecting the day's fresh catch at Captain Pete's, cooking elaborate dinners, and gathering on the deck in late afternoon for drinks and generous portions of Terry's lethal Velveeta cheese dip.

I didn't doubt that I'd know exactly the right time to release his ashes. I waited. Late afternoon of the third day, when the beach house was quiet, I placed the plastic bag filled with Terry's ashes in my backpack, along with a towel and a bottle of water. I walked along the shore to the point recalling times past when we strolled, joked, and held hands along the shoreline. I imagined Terry floating on his silver raft beyond the breakers or running to catch a *bocce* ball before it would be overtaken by the sea.

The point was deserted except for a fishing pole wedged into the sand with a line cast into the ocean. No fisherman in sight. A ribbon of seagulls flew overhead and sandpipers scurried along the water's edge. I arranged my towel a few feet from shore. Luminous pearls of sunlight shimmered over the sea's surface. Clouds fringed in orange and purple melted into a palette of mauve, peach, and rose. A mellow sunset. Yes, I thought. This is the right time and place.

I placed my backpack on top of the towel and waded ankle deep into the surf with the plastic bag in my right hand. I pinched a thimble of ashes in the palm of my hand and bent to scatter them as if I were placing marigold seeds in my garden in late spring. Then I grew bolder and hurled a handful of ashes onto the crest of a wave. Intoxicated by sun, surf, and sorrow, I twirled around and, with each rotation, flung a fistful of ashes skyward. A whirling dervish widow. When the bag was empty, I stood at the water's edge. "Well, Terry, you can rest now. You can finally rest in peace."

I picked up my pack and towel, placed the empty plastic bag in the pocket of my shorts and headed back to the beach house, where I sat on the deck staring at the ocean for a long time. I envisioned Terry beside me on the wooden rocking chair.

So it's done. You merge with the waves. But I don't know where I belong anymore. I don't know how I can go on without you.

CHAPTER FIFTEEN

Dry Land

People do not die from suicide, they die from sadness.

Anonymous

I did, in fact, gradually discover ways to go on without my husband. I devoured books on suicide and took copious notes in my journal. In *Beyond Widowhood: From Bereavement to Emergence and Hope*, Robert C. DiGiulio writes that widows whose husbands died suddenly adjusted better than those whose husbands died in ways, like suicide, that could have been prevented. I joined a widows' group and found this to be true. Every two weeks we met at an Episcopal church in a well-appointed room: high ceiling, tall windows, plush carpet, wingback chairs, love seats upholstered in tomato chintz. Imposing portraits of somber men covered the walls. Each session began with a brief introduction: widow and spouse's names, length of marriage, circumstance of spouse's death, and ages of children.

After introductions, Carrie, our compassionate leader, cautioned that our conversations should be held in strict confidence. This discretion was especially important in a small town like Charleston with its seeming two degrees of separation. She then guided us through the widow's emotional curriculum: shock, guilt, shame, anger, fear, tears, sadness, panic, resignation, acceptance, intimacy, hope, insomnia, forgetfulness, fatigue, loss of or renewed faith, and forgiveness. Like students in a biology lab, we dissected death.

We discussed the pros and cons of the anticipatory loss of our loved one through a slow, painful illness like cancer or a staggering jolt like a heart attack or aneurysm.

"We were heading for Sears in the mall. He grabbed my arm and collapsed. In seconds, he was gone. Just like that. I still can't believe it," said one stunned widow. Exactly as DiGiulio wrote, I learned that the manner of death, whether expected, or sudden, or violent, influences the grieving process.

Practical matters were addressed: funerals and memorials, headstones, wills, estates, probate, insurance, Social Security, and retirement benefits. Home repair and maintenance were high on our agenda. Almost everyone wished for "a honey, please do" male to repair the lawn mower, clean the gutters, and stop the toilet from overflowing. (Neither Terry nor I were adept at repairs, nor much interested in learning how to fix household or other items. Most often, we relied on the kindness of our engineer friends or paid large sums to repairmen.) One widow couldn't decide whether or not to purchase a new car.

"My husband traded in his Lincoln Town Car every two years." Before her husband died, he'd catalogued household chores, complete with instructions and times of the year to complete each task. One week, she knocked off two pesky jobs: cleaned the furnace filter and tackled weeds that blossomed in cracks in the driveway. Having spent the better part of one afternoon tangling with the furnace filter and resetting the pilot light on my hot water heater, I identified. Such are our meager triumphs.

With respect to discarding the deceased's personal belongings, opinions varied. The quick-to-dispose camp arranged for Goodwill to haul away coats, suits, sports jackets, shirts, cuff links, ties and their tacks, military uniforms, wrist watches, shoes, hats, scarves, gloves, jockey shorts and briefs, undershirts, pajamas, bathrobes, slippers, books, records, tools, gadgets, crutches, canes, golf clubs and bags, tennis rackets, skis, hunting rifles, fishing poles, trophies, razors, deodorant, shaving cream, and assorted medications. The not-so-fast group bided their time; others clung to everything, like refugees clutching their prized possessions. One widow left her husband's study intact, down to his pipe lying on his desk. Another established a loving ritual: Each night before going to bed, she kissed the hem of her husband's bathrobe. While I draw the line on kissing anyone's hem, occasionally I wrap myself in Terry's silk robe after a soak in a steamy bath.

Another hot topic centered on the ubiquitous wedding ring. What the heck do you do with it? Do you continue to wear it? Do you place it in your jewelry box with your class ring and charm bracelet? Do you stow it in a safe deposit box with your will, passport, and birth certificate? In face of the myriad decisions confronting the bereaved widow, the wedding ring dilemma may seem trivial. Believe me, it isn't.

Once again, choices varied. Some vowed to wear their rings forever; others adopted a wait-and-see posture. I waited. Then one evening about six months after Terry's death, I slipped my unadorned gold band off my finger and placed it on the night table beside my bed. The next morning, I tucked it into a small velvet box where it nestles still with Matt's baby bracelet and my mother's engagement ring.

Sorting through Terry's clothes was relatively easy. He didn't own much, except for hats. He'd purchased many, particularly after he began balding in his late thirties. That first year after his death, I distributed these talismans to friends and relatives: his rakish Indiana Jones number to his cousin Dinah in Dallas; his beloved Paris beret to Matt; several Irish Fishermen's caps; the gray tweed to his friend Bobby; the brown one to his mother. His battered beach hat—the straw fedora with the faded blue band—rests in the back of my bedroom closet next to the white plastic box containing the remnants of his ashes. A photo of Terry and me, with him in his straw hat, sits beside my computer as I write. His right arm is wrapped around my shoulder; my right one rests on his heart. This picture was taken at Holden Beach the summer before he died.

Several months after he died, I transferred his one good charcoal-gray suit, several sports jackets and ties, a winter parka, pants, shirts, and shoes to the closet in the guest bedroom. Torn shorts, worn socks, and sweat pants were tossed in a rag bag.

During that first year, I felt as if I was treading water trying to not drown in grief. Sometimes I'd simply cry, other times, I'd throw myself a big pity party, and on the worst days, I'd seethe in anger at Terry, as I had when he'd been drinking. I recall how late one evening in a rage over his suicide, I grabbed his worn shirts from their metal hangers and threw them on top of our bed. Brandishing pinking shears, I shredded each one, rammed the rags into a trash bag and threw them in the garbage pail. Sweet revenge. For years, I'd waged a futile campaign to banish those threadbare shirts and other fashion disasters.

"Terry, I'm packing some boxes for Goodwill. Why don't you throw out a few of those old shirts? They're practically in tatters. Why not sort through our closet and weed out the worst?"

"Frannie, don't mess with my shirts. They're perfectly good. They're comfortable. Besides, I only wear them around the house."

Sometimes I'd sneak a few into the Goodwill bag. Once, while rummaging through a box of my giveaways, he retrieved his dingy white, terrycloth pants, which were four inches too short and held together with a draw string at the waist. "Why are you throwing out my beach pants?" he asked.

"Because you look like a goober in them. They're embarrassing."

"Foiled again, Frannie," he chuckled as he waved those pants above his head, like an Olympic star brandishing his gold medal.

Although the widows' group sustained me after Terry's death, I often felt "apart from." Those who had nursed their husbands through long illnesses, like cancer and Alzheimer's, had had time to prepare for death. Suicide didn't compromise their loss. Even in this enlightened era, suicide carries a stigma, a legacy from the time when cadavers were dragged, hanged by their feet, burned, and thrown into the refuse pile, destined to hell. In England, the bodies were placed under the high road, pinned to the ground, with a stake driven through the chest. It wasn't too long ago that the bodies of suicide victims were set apart from others in cemeteries. The stigma remains. It's impossible for the uninitiated to comprehend. The other widows shared my sorrow, but not my shame. We swam in different pools.

Moreover, many praised their husbands in what one writer labels "spouse sanctification." The widow idealizes the image of her deceased husband, as if to prove she had the good sense to choose an unblemished partner.

Unlike the others, I couldn't revere Terry. He wasn't a candidate for sainthood like Mother Teresa. When the wives genuflected before their husbands, I felt guilty. Curiously, the widows praised their Harrys, Bobs, and Joes in the present verb tense.

"He's the salt of the earth; he never meets a stranger; he's a loving grandpa, a terrific father, a dedicated son, a faithful companion."

"My husband is kind, compassionate, caring, tender and talented. He's the love of my life and my best friend."

"I can't imagine life without him."

Dashing in their youth and wise in their golden years, these paragons were candidates for beatification. At least it seemed so to me.

Venerating the dead is one thing; deconstructing the death of a depressed soul is another. Since we respect the dead, it's unseemly to feel ambivalent or, worse yet, to feel relieved. I recall the shock of recognition when I read that the majority of widows of husbands who abused alcohol and other drugs admitted relief that the suicide brought an end to the misery of all concerned. Did that fact apply to me?

While Terry's death freed me from the-day-to-day challenges of living with an alcoholic, it caged me in guilt. How was I to reconcile the split between my grief and relief? Did his death free me? Did it free both of us? Would my life be easier without him? If so, dare I admit it?

In our death-phobic society, we shun grief and recoil from suicide.

But grief needs an audience. It craves attention. It thrives on the love and support of family, friends, neighbors, acquaintances, and coworkers. The bereaved applaud those treasured souls who phone, send cards, hold their hands, wipe away their tears, bake casseroles, pick up laundry, mail, and groceries, and help sort through mountains of legal and financial paperwork. Above all, the bereaved prize those who listen.

They prize those who listen without an agenda, who don't offer advice. ("Maybe you should go spend some time with your sister in New York.")

Who don't mouth platitudes. ("It's God's will. In time this will pass.")

Who don't compare. ("Do you remember my cousin, Millie? The one who lives in Colorado. She lost a brother to colon cancer and a father to Alzheimer's in the same year.")

And who don't consider grief to be a quick trip through the express checkout line and insist that the bereaved "get over it and move on."

Grief is as individual as a thumb print. At every widows' meeting, Carrie said, "Everyone grieves differently, in her own way at her own pace." There's no straight line. We zig and we zag. While grief has no timetable, experts estimate that the gut-wrenching variety should abate after two years. If not, the mourner should seek professional help.

During that first winter, my fatigue was punishing. I felt as if I cradled a boulder of grief in my arms. Each day, I knotted fetal on the living room couch. Shrouded in a heavy blanket, I listened to soulful sounds of Tom Waits and Julee Cruise. I cried, sometimes for hours at a stretch. In time, the fatigue lifted and the grief shifted to sadness. And, sometimes anger. Though less frequent, the tears still remain at times.

Grief is relentless and provides no respite. When I slept, I dreamt of Terry. When awake, I thought of him constantly. In-between were the apparitions. One day, his beat-up Plymouth Fury pulled in front of me on Kanawha Turnpike. *That car's too old to be on the road, I thought.* Another day, a late model van sporting a vanity "Van Gogh" license plate idled in front of me at a traffic light. (Don McLean's "Vincent," written about Van Gogh, was one of the songs played at Terry's memorial.) One evening, his beat-up leather satchel tumbled from a shelf in the bedroom closet to the floor. Tucked in the pocket of one of his sports jackets, I discovered a wrinkled copy of W. H. Auden's poem, "Funeral Blues" that had been cut out of a newspaper. He must have saved it from a movie review of *Four Weddings and a Funeral,* which was released in 1994. I remember how we howled at scenes in that movie. Even today, when the wind chimes flutter outside the window in my study, I seem to hear his gentle voice.

Then there were nightmares and strange dreams.

I vividly recall two that I recorded in my journal. One was set in the circus:

I'm on a TV or movie set, I can't tell where exactly. There are actors all around: Robert Mitchum, Peter Fonda, Milton Berle, and Robert Ryan (two tough guys, one comic, and an "easy rider." Definitely a telling cast of characters). In the distance, I see Terry in a tent, a circus tent. It's canary yellow. He's dressed in a black bowler hat, like Chaplin's Little Tramp. The tent is far away, but I can see him clearly. He's alive and I remember thinking, How remarkable. He's alive and he's feeling. The actors begin to perform, each standing in a separate circle under a spotlight, like a juggler in one ring in the circus tent. "Ladies and gentlemen and here..." I feel angry because he didn't tell me he was going to perform. He pretended to be dead. He lied to me again.

I catch up with him and try to comfort him. I'm confused and upset, but also ecstatic that he's alive. I feel like a mother who finds a missing child; she's joyful but angry because he strayed far from where he was supposed to be.

"Why did you pretend to be dead?" I asked.

"I did it for you. I was going anyway. Suicide was just insurance. I didn't want to hurt you anymore. No choice. Best like this.

Another dream was set in the Rocky Mountains.

I'm at the YMCA camp in Estes Park, Colorado, out walking with my friend Jeanne on a brilliant blue-sky day. We enter the main lodge, a huge stone building with timber beams framing a vaulted ceiling. An elk head hangs over the

*hearth of an enormous fireplace on the far end of the room.
I walk toward a long, knotty pine counter. A reservation
clerk grabs my hand and whispers, "Hurry, he's going to
die very soon. We put him in a small room near the General
Store, second door to the left." I squeeze her hand and
mutter, "Thank you." Neither surprised nor frightened, I
walk toward the room to rescue him again.*

*I find Terry face down on a gurney with his left leg
hanging over the side, like a slab of raw beef. I crouch
down beside him; my fingertips touch the soft hair above
the base of his spine. His body is warm; it is always warm.
He stirs slightly and begins to roll off the gurney. I grab
him but can't break his fall. He lies motionless on the floor,
his body folds fetal, like an unborn baby cushioned in his
mother's womb. I slide my right hand under his face and
lift it toward me. I draw back. Each of his eyes has two
irises, one beside the other: hazel, his natural color, to the
right, and blood red, to the left. I stare. My eyes are as
vacant as his are damaged.*

I couldn't get back to sleep after that dream.

At the end of January, when classes started back up, I was
physically, emotionally, and intellectually unprepared. My dean
encouraged me to take as much time off as I needed. I opted to
return to the daily stream of preparing for classes, sorting through
paperwork, and interacting with colleagues and students to
redirect my unremitting grief. I anticipated awkward moments.
*What if I break down in front of my coworkers or, worse yet, my
students? How would my colleagues react to Terry's suicide? Would
they pity me? Would they avoid me? Would they think that I could have
prevented his death? Would they judge or condemn me? And what
would I say if someone asked how my husband died?* (In time, I settled

on this strategy: When strangers inquired as to the cause of death, I replied: "It was sudden and unexpected." If they pressed, which most didn't, I'd say suicide. Thus, I didn't hide nor did I volunteer the truth.)

That first day back to school I hid in my office, sorted through mail, and outlined a "to do" list for the coming weeks. Before leaving, I posted an email to thank everyone for their cards, phone calls, and flowers. I asked for prayers and hugs and included the verse that I wrote for Terry's memorial:

> Husband of a Thousand Joys and Sorrows
>
> Wave in ocean
>
> Soul in motion
>
> Leaf in flight
>
> Released from demons
>
> Resting with angels
>
> Forever
>
> In eternal light
>
> Ciao, Frannie

When I returned home each day, I crawled onto the couch and covered myself in sorrow. In the ensuing months, my coworkers offered pats on my back and soothing words. I remember how James, who occupied the office next to mine, wrapped his burly arms around me.

"How ya doin', Fran? Need anything? Just stick your head in the door. I'm right here for you." His bear hugs helped sustain me.

A few coworkers averted their eyes from me in the elevator or at the photocopy machine. On my first day back, one of the guys who worked in the print shop looked away as he passed me in the hall. Months later he apologized.

"I'm sorry, I didn't know what to say, and I didn't want to upset you."

This seemingly insensitive behavior rests on the false assumption that speaking of the dead upsets the living, especially in the case of suicide. Suicide survivors experience a triple whammy. We grieve for our loved one, we suffer from the trauma, and we endure the silence of those who don't want to talk about it.

Although I mourned with other widows, my husband's suicide set me apart. I felt I needed a different kind of support. On September 21, 1997, I headed west on I-64 to Louisville, Kentucky, to the Pathways to Healing Conference for survivors of suicide. As I passed horses grazing in gentle bluegrass country, I recalled our trips to Keeneland Racetrack where Terry studied a racing form as if he were preparing for the state bar exam. He liked to place bets on oddball combinations: exactas, quinellas, and trifectas.

"Terry, I don't understand all these complicated formulas you come up with. Why can't you bet to win, place, or show, like my father and his cronies?"

"No offense, but that's too easy," he'd wink. "And not enough fun."

He'd review the racing form, and then scrutinize the tote board calculating the odds. (I opted for a less scientific approach, placing my two-dollar bets on the name of a horse, color of the jockey's silks, or number at the starting gate.) Right before post time, he'd rush to lock in his bets. After a few races, he'd load up on hot dogs, fries, peanuts, popcorn, and Dr. Peppers.

"I got you a dog with mustard. No onions, no chili, no slaw, no special sauce. You Yankees don't know what you're missing. You want some fries with ketchup?" While he cheered for his favorites, he never screamed or shouted. Win or lose, he enjoyed his day at the races.

"Hard to beat the ponies, Frannie. But it's fun trying."

When I arrived in Louisville, I headed for Saint Matthew's Episcopal Church, where, like shipwreck survivors, seventy lost souls sought a day's solace from sorrow. At the registration desk, each survivor was given a "relationship loss ribbon": light blue for a son, pink for a daughter, green for husband, yellow for wife, royal blue for father, orange for mother, tan for brother, lavender for sister, and white for a friend or other. A rainbow of grief filled the room. (My green ribbon is pinned to the bulletin board above my desk as I write.)

The keynote speaker discussed research findings: What we know and need to know about suicide. Risk factors include genetics and low levels of serotonin. Loss, failure, or other disappointments—grief, divorce, unemployment, as well as severe depression, anxiety, or psychosis result in loss of faith and acts of self-destruction. One-third of all suicides and one-quarter of all attempts are committed by alcoholics, like Terry. They're at special risk, particularly during a crisis.

I later learned that Terry had indeed faced such a crisis because his driver's license had been suspended two weeks before he died. About two weeks after Terry's death, our State Farm agent phoned and asked, "Didn't you know he had been in a car wreck, Fran?" In fact, I didn't. A few days later when going through Terry's papers, I discovered two letters. The first was from the West Virginia Department of Motor Vehicles notifying Terry that his driver's license would be suspended. It was dated December 14, 1996, eleven days before his suicide. The second was written by Terry requesting a hearing to reinstate his license. It was dated December 16, 1996.

In addition to crisis, the speaker touched upon survivors' three main challenges: anger and guilt and the ubiquitous "why?" Like archeologists, survivors dig for clues to shed light on possible causes. "Why" haunts us, sometimes for a lifetime. *Why, when I loved, nurtured, and cared for Terry, did he abandon me? Why didn't the holiday spirit move me to forgive rather than berate him? Why, when Terry confessed that he'd messed up again, did I shoot back: 'Terry, you used up your messing-up quota a long time ago.' I choke on guilt when I recall that last conversation on Christmas morning.*

Our society harbors the illusion that suicide is rare when, in fact, someone in America commits suicide every seventeen minutes. The speaker ended with this caution: "It's not possible to make sense out of suicide and to know what someone was thinking while committing the act."

Next, a panel of four survivors told their stories. After her teenage son's suicide, a mother said, "I couldn't believe it. Suicide didn't happen to families like mine." In fact, suicide, like addiction, doesn't discriminate among gender, race, age, social class, geographical area, or religious or political affiliation.

After lunch, we gathered in the church basement in breakout groups. I selected "How Your Personal Relationship to the Victim Affects Your Grief Process as a Survivor." It seemed to cover all bases. Eight of us wearing different color ribbons pushed metal chairs together in a tight circle. Free from the burden of hiding our stigma, shock, shame, and silence, we unloaded our sorrow like weary travelers at the end of an arduous journey. One woman wore three ribbons: green for her ex-husband, light blue for her son, and white for an old boyfriend, all alcoholics. A young husband, who wore a yellow ribbon, sang the first note of our if-only chorus of guilt and regret. "If only I had insisted she see a psychiatrist for her depression." The rest of us took up the beat. "If only I hadn't gone out of town that weekend." "If only I took his threats seriously." "If only I had been more loving . . . compassionate . . . sensitive . . . observant . . . aware."

If only we were clairvoyant.

In that safe space, we spewed out details about the particular methods our loved ones chose to end their lives. One young woman's fiancée shot himself in front of her. Her dark eyes flashed as she described globs of brain matter and blood splattered on the walls, floor, bedspread, and curtains of her bedroom. "My sister helped me clean it up. It took us two days." A young mother of a four-month-old daughter discovered her husband's mutilated body in their bedroom. "The people he worked with say he shot himself because he didn't want the baby. They blame me." The mother of two teens discovered her husband's body hanging from a noose on a rope wrapped around a hook in the ceiling of their laundry room. "Thank God, the children weren't home at the time." A middle-aged man drove his pickup to a fishing stream, doused himself with gasoline, and set himself on fire. His widow said, "We were having problems. We had a fight that morning." One victim died from carbon monoxide poisoning, another ingested antifreeze. A soft-spoken country woman in her sixties, the mother of three sons, shared that the youngest, an addict, had shot himself in their bathroom. Her husband and other two sons refused to talk about it. Even in this high-tech world, the old methods—firearms, stabbing, pills, gas, and hanging—still prevail, with gunshots accounting for 60 percent of all suicides.

No one mentioned death by suffocation, nor did I. This clean and efficient method is recommended in Derek Humphrey's *Final Exit*, first published in 1991. If Terry had planned his death, had he read that book? Or was he familiar with physician Sherwin Nuland's *How We Die, Reflections on Life's Final Chapter* that describes how someone swallows sleeping pills and then encloses his head in a tightly sealed plastic bag. The oxygen gets used up quickly. The low blood-oxygen level crashes the heart quickly, resulting in death.

What had the moment of not being alive been for Terry? Or the moment right before that? Did he say to himself, "Soon I will be dead?" Did he think of me as he took his last breath?

To piece together the events of Terry's final hours, I requested paperwork from his stay at the hospital. I learned later that on Christmas Day the police found him passed out in his car in the parking lot near his office building. He was then rushed to Charleston Area Medical Center. The nurses' log helped me put together the puzzle pieces of his last hours. The first entry was written at 1:09 p.m.

> This 47 year-old found in automobile unresponsive EMS reports upon arrival pt (patient) difficult to arouse/used ammonia caps. Pt upon arrival drowsy, assist getting undressed and place on monitor.

He tried to get out of bed and pulled the IV out of his arm. The log noted:

> Soft wrist restraints applied to prevent pt from harming himself. Pt continues to try to get out of bed.

He pulled out the restraints; the restraints were reapplied. This yanking back and forth continued until 6:30 p.m., when the log noted:

> Pt attempts to contact a sober family member to come after him.

That sober family member wasn't me. At 7:15 p.m., he was discharged to go home with a friend:

> Verbal instructions given to the pt and friend and acknowledgement of understanding.

Acknowledge what? Understand what? He was wheeled out the front door to a car.

It turned out that Terry's lawyer friend, Robin, had come after him at the hospital. He called me the day after Terry died.

"He seemed a little ragged," Robin told me. "I offered to drive him home, but he said he wanted to go to his office. We talked, for a long time. He was awfully worried about the DUI, brought it up again and again. I assured him that we'd take care of it. He also talked about getting drunk on Christmas Eve. He seemed to believe that you wouldn't forgive him. I offered to drive him home again, but he said he needed time to recover. He assured me that he was okay. I asked if he wanted me to call you. He said he'd call later. I left him at his office around ten or so. I feel awful."

"It's not your fault, and I'm glad you were with him."

The hospital toxicology test registered ethyl alcohol level of 0.452, which is perilously over the 0.008 legal limit, or as his good friend PC observed, "My God. That's enough to kill a horse." Most likely, Terry was in a blackout when he pulled that plastic bag over his head and crossed into formless spirit.

If we die as we live, then Terry's method reflected his quiet, unassuming personality. Shooting, stabbing, or hanging weren't his style.

In another workshop session at the suicide conference, we explored our guilt. "Why didn't we recognize the warning signs?" "Why didn't we take threats seriously?" "Why didn't we insist that our spouses be hospitalized?" "Why didn't we return that last phone call?" Survivors hold themselves responsible. Their guilt is compounded because others see the suicide as preventable. "Surely more could have been done," they whisper.

Did I, too, fail to recognize telltale signs? Perhaps so.

Three months before Terry's death, on a golden autumn afternoon, I had stood in front a class of sixth graders during my weekly visit to their classroom, and read a chapter of *Tuck Everlasting*. (Ironically, the novel's theme deals with the conundrum of immortality.) Halfway through the reading, the school secretary entered and whispered to Ms. Von, the classroom teacher, who then motioned to me.

"There's been a call. An emergency at your house." I grabbed my book bag and purse. Twenty-five sets of curious eyes followed my progress as I fled the room.

When I pulled into the driveway of our new home, a middle aged man in khaki pants and a denim shirt greeted me.

"Don't be frightened. Your husband isn't hurt; he's sleeping on the couch inside." This stranger explained that he lived with the woman who'd purchased our old house, which was a few blocks away from our new one. Earlier that afternoon, he'd found Terry sitting on the patio, staring ahead, blank and uncommunicative. But the man recognized Terry, drove him home and settled him down.

"I'm a doctor, and his vitals are okay. He needs to sleep it off. Do you want me to stay for a while?"

"No," I replied. "Are you sure that he doesn't need to go to the emergency room or something?"

"He's okay, he needs to sleep it off. He left his car in our driveway. Don't worry about it; come over to get it when you can. You or someone else needs to stay with him. Don't leave him alone."

Terry didn't rouse. I covered him with a blanket and phoned Eleanor, our therapist. "Don't panic," she said. "Is he out cold?"

"Yes."

"Then he'll probably sleep the rest of the day. I'll clear my appointments for you. Come in first thing tomorrow morning. Whatever you do, don't leave him alone."

Months before this incident, in the aftermath of another binge, I'd yelled: "Terry, can't you see, we're heading for a crisis. And I don't know how to prevent it. I'm scared, seriously scared."

"Frannie, you're overreacting again. It's a little bump in the road. We'll be fine."

"No, this is serious. We have to do something. Maybe we should see a therapist again. I'm utterly at a loss and don't know what to do anymore. We need someone to help us." After twenty years of coping with addiction, I still harbored hope and sailed on the illusion that therapy would keep us afloat. Such is the deadly power of denial.

A few days passed. Terry made excuses; I persisted. Finally to placate me, he agreed. We embarked on another round of therapy, this time with Eleanor, a forthright Southerner with a keen sense of humor, like Lenny.

Once again, we described our drama: binges and blackouts, tears and reconciliations, pleas and promises, catastrophes and catharses, my codependence, his guilt and shame. We oscillated between pleasure and pain, hope and despair.

When twelve-step groups were mentioned, Terry dodged. "I know it's a good program, but I can't get past all of the Higher Power, God stuff. Besides, I've gone to a few meetings but I don't feel comfortable."

"There are many groups. At least twenty meet in the valley at one time or another every week," I countered.

Eleanor interrupted. "If you aren't comfortable with the Twelve Steps, there are alternative programs; they go by different names. It's different from traditional twelve-step programs. They were designed for the rationally inclined rather than spiritually inclined. Sounds like one might work for you." She turned in her swivel chair to ruffle through her files and pulled out a flyer with the name of a local contact. Terry feigned interest.

For the next few weeks, I nagged. "Did you call that number Eleanor gave us? Are any meetings scheduled soon? I'd be happy to go with you if it's an open program." He promised to "look into it." He never did. Weary from our tug of war, I didn't press any further, at least not then.

For too many years, I'd waged a relentless campaign to fix my husband. In fact, as chief enabler and codependent, I had my own problems but failed to acknowledge them. My "God suit" fit like a second skin and I enjoyed wearing it.

The therapist aims for abstinence, the enabler for control of the addict, and the addict for control over alcohol or other drugs. Many addicts experience a honeymoon during which they can control use—usually for five to ten years. Long after they lose their self-respect, many hang onto their jobs, their family, and their relationships despite setbacks and reversals. I find it remarkable that Terry's and my tattered marriage held together until the end. Then again, we were as addicted to one another as a junkie to heroin. Our drama made us feel alive.

The morning after Terry's blackout, we drove to Eleanor's office in silence. We took our respective seats in identical yellow-upholstered, check-patterned wingback chairs. A crystal bowl of hard candy and box of Kleenex sat on top of the mahogany table between us. Eleanor, in her denim jumper and sensible shoes, sat across the room in a swivel chair. As we talked, she jotted notes on a pad attached to a clipboard.

Starved for sympathy, I shoved my fork into Terry's bowl and recounted the previous day's events. Terry said little. No doubt he tried to mollify me, minimize the damage, and vowed to try harder. At one point, Eleanor speculated that Terry might have been caught in a "fugue" state when he landed on the patio. "Fugue" is a euphemism for blackout.

The autumn colors faded. The trees shed their leaves. The weather turned cold. Therapy continued. The blackouts accelerated. The crisis passed. And then Terry killed himself. A week later on a blue cold morning, I returned to Eleanor's office where I sank into a check-patterned wingback chair with an empty heart and a soul full of despair. Thus, I began my long journey of survival.

DARK WINE WATERS

CHAPTER SIXTEEN

Clear Sailing

I am not afraid of storms for
I am learning how to sail my ship.

Louisa May Alcott

Several years after Terry died, once again I headed into rough seas.

My son Matt had drifted for several years, living on the margins. Eventually he returned to Charleston, and I discovered that he was addicted to drugs. Although he'd ostensibly moved back in with me, he'd be gone for days, crashed in some apartment with his addict friends. He'd check back in at home to borrow money, wash clothes, and get a free meal. We'd argue. I'd plead with him to get help. No dice. Finally, I kicked him out. He landed in a homeless shelter.

I climbed back onto my "pity pot" and cursed God and the universe for this unbearable burden. *How could this have happened again? What did I do to deserve this? What if he died from a drug overdose? Or committed suicide like Terry?*

I couldn't let that happen. Not again. My panic attacks returned. I lost weight and couldn't sleep. I functioned on autopilot at work, preparing for my classes, interacting with colleagues, and grading student papers. Whenever Matt called with a problem, I'd fly out of my office door to rescue him. Once when he called to borrow money again, I screamed at him. A colleague who was passing by in the hallway asked, "Are you all right?" I broke down and cried.

After all of these years with Terry, I still would not accept that I was powerless over a loved one's addiction. I was terrified that Matt also might die from the disease. So I intervened time after time, year after year, crisis after crisis. Talk about a slow learner!

In utter despair, I confided in a friend who's an addiction counselor. She urged me to try a recovery program specifically for family members. "I'm worried about you. You're a wreck. I think that a twelve-step program could help. Go to a few meetings. Give it a try. I'll get you a schedule."

"I went to a few meetings when Terry was alive. It didn't seem right for me. All that talk about surrendering to a Higher Power. I don't know. Maybe I should try a therapist. That might help."

A few months later, I received a phone call to tell me that my son had been arrested for check rendering. I panicked and bailed him out of jail. Despite this criminal charge, Matt didn't hit bottom.

But I did.

I reconsidered going to recovery meetings again. *I'm comfortable in groups and don't panic when I walk into a room of strangers. But what if I break down and cry in front of strangers? That's different from introducing myself and schmoozing. Additionally, Charleston is a small town. I run into people all the time, especially my former students. What if one of them is there?* But I pushed aside my reservations and dug out the meeting schedule. At seven the next evening, I drove to a church.

Although many in recovery recall the day, month, and year of their first meeting, I don't. But I do remember that it was summer because it was light enough for me to walk along the river afterward. Being close to water always calms me.

At the meeting, a woman approached me with a smile.

"Are you a newcomer?" I nodded. "Welcome. See me after the meeting and I'll give you a packet of information and some phone numbers if you want them." The room was crowded. When I sat down, I recognized one of my former students. She sat directly across from me at a large rectangular table. *My luck*. We nodded. Signs were scattered around the table.

"Live and Let Live."

"One Day at a Time."

"Let Go and Let God."

"What You Say Here Stays Here."

The meeting began. Each member took a turn reading one of the Twelve Steps. *Okay, so far. I'm familiar with the steps from the treatment center*. Then readings from two or three books. A brief run-through of the format and suggested topic. The leader turned to me. "You don't have to share when it's your turn. You can pass."

I can't remember the topic, but I do remember that a guy with a baseball cap "ran his mouth." Each person said her name, addressed the topic, and ended with "I pass." No interruptions or cross talk. Many passes. Then my turn. I couldn't even say my name. Instead, I cried. Someone handed me a tissue, and then I passed.

Everyone seemed to speak from the heart. There was pain, but laughter, too. And stories like mine: sons, daughters, and spouses addicted to alcohol and other drugs. No one mentioned suicide, but the long, slow suicide of active addiction was the reason we all were there. At the meeting's closing, we stood up, joined hands, and recited the Serenity Prayer, with a tiny squeeze of fingers and shake of hands at the end.

"Keep coming back. It works when you work it. So work it 'cause you're worth it."

Then folks stood chatting in pairs and small groups. More laughter. Many hugs. The woman who had greeted me said, "It takes courage to get here. I hope you'll keep coming back." She suggested that I try six meetings and then decide whether the program might work for me. She handed me a packet of information, with a schedule for different meetings, offered her phone number, and gave me a hug. "I hope you'll come back."

I kept going back.

At first, I was put off by some slogans.

"Easy does it."

"Keep it simple."

"One day at a time."

They seemed *too* simple, too trite. Addiction is too cunning and complicated. How can anyone keep their life simple in the face of such chaos? But one slogan, "Listen and learn," made sense. During those initial meetings, I didn't say much but I did learn many helpful aspects of recovery. One of the first concepts that I learned was the meaning of the "three Cs." I didn't cause it. I can't control it. And I can't cure it. Like a mantra, members repeat this often, especially to newcomers.

I felt responsible for having somehow caused my son's addiction, much as I felt guilt for Terry's suicide. What had I done or not done during Matt's formative years? I'd read enough psychology to know that divorcing Matt's father and marrying an alcoholic had to have had a profound influence on my son. After all, they were his male role models. I questioned my decision to move to West Virginia. Would Matt have become closer to his father if I remained in Chapel Hill? I questioned my parenting style. Was I too permissive? Too distracted with Terry to give Matt enough attention? Or was I in denial when Matt kept running out of money, making excuses for losing jobs, and associating with people I didn't know? My Catholic guilt swept over me like a monster wave. If only I had been a better mother, none of this would have happened. In those early days of my recovery, hearing the phrase "I didn't cause it" provided me comfort.

The second C, "I can't control it" was the most difficult. Adrift in an island of fear, I tried to prevent the next crisis. I injected myself into my son's life the way a nurse jabs a needle into a patient's arm. The medicine didn't take, but that didn't deter me.

I poked and prodded. "Did you remember to phone the unemployment office? Do you have clean clothes? Did you renew your driver's license? Did you buy any groceries with the money I gave you? Did you have the oil changed in your car? Did you call the doctor to get your prescription refilled?"

"Don't worry. I'll pay that speeding ticket, that cell-phone bill, that car payment, that student loan."

"By the way, one of my friends called about a part-time job. Don't forget to call him back. Here's the number."

"Maybe you should consider going back to school. The semester's starting soon. I can make an appointment for you with a counselor at the admission office."

When Matt ran out of cash, I replenished it. When he bounced a check, I covered it. When he landed in jail, I bailed him out. When he stole money from my wallet, I ignored it. When he didn't contact me for a week or two, I searched the seedy part of town, where the junkies and prostitutes hang out on street corners. I snooped around the homeless shelter and free soup kitchen. I called friends. And my heart raced whenever the phone rang in the middle of the night.

All of this was in vain, but I didn't know it at the time. My son was addicted to drugs and I was addicted to my son. A classic codependent.

I dislike that word. It's difficult to define and has leeched into our collective vocabulary, like its cousin "dysfunctional." However, everyone I've encountered in my recovery group has struggled to become free from controlling and trying to manage the addict's life. To get the hell out of the way. To keep our forks in our own plates. To walk on our side of the street. To mind our own damn business. We think that if we try hard enough, yell loud enough, and nag long enough, eventually our loved ones will wake up, stop using, and seek recovery. Although this is as futile as trying to stop the rain from falling, we persist.

The need to relinquish control is implied in the Serenity Prayer.

"God grant me the courage to accept the things I cannot change . . ." It's in the first of the Twelve Steps, "We admitted we were powerless . . . that our lives had become unmanageable."

The third C, "I can't cure it" was difficult to grasp. Addiction is a disease with a genetic component that puts certain individuals, like my husband and my son, at higher risk than those who lack the genetics of addiction. The only cure is to stop using, to abstain entirely from the behaviors and substances that can lead to death. Not only is there a physical component, such as blackouts and mood swings, there's a psychological one as well. Behaviors such as denial get tossed into the mix. Add the codependent's intractable belief that she can "cure" the addict and you have a recipe for tragedy.

One of my favorite stories, which always gets a knowing laugh at meetings, is about pigeons. A man sat under a tree full of pigeons. The pigeons did what they do best. The man shouted at them and thundered away. But then he realized that the pigeons were doing what they do because they were pigeons and not because he happened to be under the tree at the time. Addicts will do what they do best: they drink and drug. And, loved ones, like the man who sat under the tree, shout, nag, and berate them instead of letting go and getting out of their way.

Although I can't cure my son, I can take care of myself. I have choices. I can either struggle against the riptide of obsession, shame, guilt, fear, self-pity, self-righteousness, resentment, denial, and anger or head toward safer waters. As one member said, "Fran, all you have to do is to be willing."

Several years ago, on a trip to St. Croix, I took a sailing lesson and discovered that although I have, as I stated at the beginning of this tale, always lived my life in currents, I wasn't cut out to be a sailor. I wasn't adept at handling the rudder, tying knots, or lowering the boom so that it didn't hit me on my head. Although enchanted with the idea of sailing, I wasn't willing to put forth the time and effort to learn the basics.

Not so with my twelve-step fellowship. I was in so much pain that I was willing to try almost anything. I kept going back. I listened and learned.

I learned that I can't fix my son's problems. Unless an addict experiences the consequences of his bad choices and poor decisions (and the sooner the better), he won't recover. My sponsor often reminds me that every time I bailed my son out of a financial or legal mess, I robbed him of the opportunity to build up his self-confidence and kept him from the consequences of his own acts. I learned that working a twelve-step program encompasses more than only dealing with the addicts. The principles and slogans, such as, "One day at a time," and "Live and let live," are helpful in day-to-day interactions with friends, coworkers, even strangers. And they sure come in handy during a crisis.

I learned not to berate myself over past behavior (especially after completing my Fourth Step inventory). As I relived my journey with Terry in this story, I felt shame, guilt, and regret for what I said and did. At the time, I didn't know better. Now that I know better, I try to do better.

I learned that expectations can result in resentment; faith counteracts fear; humility isn't a four letter word; and that it's okay to mourn lost hopes and dreams.

Of the Seven Capital Sins in Dante's *Inferno*, envy, along with anger and pride, perverts love. The envious were among those farthest away from Paradise. Even with their eyes sewn shut, they weep over their sins. Although I see clearly how envy and self-pity diminish me, like a narcotic, they seduce me. Giving up smoking was easy compared to letting go of feeling sorry for myself. I found pitying myself more comforting than a slow drag on a Salem Menthol.

Heavy doses of gratitude help mitigate self-pity and other character defects. Today I am grateful for my fulfilling career, my loving and faithful family and friends, my fourteen-year-old Westie, Woody, and the blessing of recovery, both mine and my son's. Most especially, I am grateful for the opportunity to share my story and offer hope to those challenged by their loved one's addiction.

Working a twelve-step program hasn't been easy. After many years of attending meetings, reading program literature, and working the steps, I still fumble, exactly as I did during that sailing lesson long ago. Then my sponsor reminds me to set my sights on progress, not perfection. So I reverse course and point my compass toward the sun and navigate toward serenity.